PRAYING GOD'S PROMISES IN TOUGH TIMES

PRAYING
GOD'S PROMISES
in TOUGH TIMES

Len Woods

Tyndale House Publishers, Inc.
Wheaton, Illinois

Visit Tyndale's exciting Web site at www.tyndale.com

Praying God's Promises in Tough Times

Copyright © 2002 by Len Woods. All rights reserved.

Cover illustration by Julie Chen. Copyright © 2002 by Tyndale House Publishers. All rights reserved.

Author photo copyright © by Allison Peatross, Picture This, Inc. All rights reserved.

Designed by Julie Chen

Edited by Susan Taylor

Scripture quotations are taken from the *Holy Bible,* New Living Translation, copyright © 1996. Used by permission of Tyndale House Publishers, Inc., Wheaton, Illinois 60189. All rights reserved.

Library of Congress Cataloging-in-Publication Data

Woods, Len.
  Praying God's promises in tough times / Len Woods.
    p. cm.
Includes index.
  ISBN 0-8423-6006-9
  1. God—Promises—Prayer-books and devotions—English. 2. God—Promises—Biblical teaching.
3. Christian life—Biblical teaching. I. Title.
  BT180.P7 W66 2002
  242′.4—dc21   2002002846

Printed in the United States of America

08 07 06 05 04 03 02
7   6   5   4   3   2   1

TO CHRIST COMMUNITY CHURCH OF RUSTON

THERE IS NO GROUP OF SAINTS ANYWHERE

THAT I'D RATHER BE WITH ON THIS JOURNEY—

ESPECIALLY WHEN TIMES ARE TOUGH.

YOU COULD HAVE WRITTEN THIS BOOK—

AND I SUPPOSE IN MANY WAYS, YOU DID.

PART 2: LOOKING UP: THE GOD WE SERVE

PART 3: LOOKING WITHIN:
THE RESOURCES WE HAVE

PART 4: LOOKING AHEAD:
THE FUTURE WE SEE

CONTENTS

SPECIAL THANKS GO TO:

JON FARRAR, SUE TAYLOR, AND ALL THE OTHER TALENTED FOLKS
AT TYNDALE, FOR ALLOWING ME TO PARTNER WITH YOU IN THIS PROJECT.
I APPRECIATE YOUR LOVE FOR WORDS AND ESPECIALLY GOD'S WORDS.
I MARVEL AT BOTH YOUR PASSION AND YOUR ABILITY TO COMMUNICATE
TRUTH IN SUCH CREATIVE AND PRACTICAL WAYS.

CINDI, WALTER, AND JACK. YOU MAKE MY LIFE—EVEN THE
NOT-SO-FUN PARTS—RICH AND SATISFYING.

THE ELDER/STAFF TEAM AT CCC. I DON'T SAY IT ENOUGH,
BUT YOU ARE THE BEST, MOST TALENTED GROUP OF FOLKS AROUND.

DAVE VEERMAN AND BRUCE BARTON OF THE LIVINGSTONE CORPORATION.
WHERE WOULD I BE WITHOUT YOUR ENCOURAGEMENT?

THE GUYS WHO TRY TO KEEP ME SANE AND POINTED IN THE
RIGHT DIRECTION. YOU KNOW WHO YOU ARE.

THIS book is about three things.

First, it's about the tough times of life—*your* life. The fact that you're reading this page suggests that you've moved from the naive question of, How do I avoid pain and hardship? to the more mature and realistic dilemma of, When tragedy and turmoil *do* come my way, how should I respond?

Second, this is a book about praying. Each page contains an honest, heartfelt petition. All these prayers are rooted in the divine assurances of Scripture. None of them are magic. They're meant only to serve as guides, to help you put in words the pain and confusion deep in your soul.

Last and most important, this is a book of promises— 120 passages from the pages of the Bible that describe vividly who God is, what he's like, what he says to you in times of crisis, and what he does for you.

The great danger of books like this (i.e., little books about huge problems and mysteries) is that they have the potential to come across as glib and hokey. Let's face it, when our lives are falling apart, the last thing we want is a collection of perky little platitudes. But we *do* need truth. Which is precisely what God's Word is (John 17:17) and precisely why the promises of God take center stage in these pages.

Praying God's Promises in Tough Times is a modest attempt to point those who hurt back to what God has said. It doesn't claim to be a quick fix for your problems. It likely will not take away your sorrow. But if you deeply ponder the promises it spotlights, they *will* bring you face-to-face with almighty God himself. And that's a place where miraculous things can and do happen.

Before you dive in, let me clarify a few things:

First, this book uses the word *promise* not only in the strict sense of a specific divine pledge of what will be but also in the broader sense of a theological truth regarding what is. For example, in devotion 66, the featured promise is from John 10:10, which reads, "My purpose is to give life in all its fullness." Notice this verse doesn't so much guarantee that Jesus will do something for us in the days and weeks ahead as it reminds us what Christ would like to do for us and in us. It is not so much a "promise" (in the technical sense of the term) as it is a reassuring statement of divine desire—a passage upon which we can stand and be confident.

Second, beware of the common tendency to consider *every* divine promise or pronouncement (including those made in historically unique situations) as directly applicable to your life.

For example, I once knew a well-meaning believer who "felt led by God" to form a Christian sports team. He "claimed" Habakkuk 2:2-3 as a heavenly guarantee that his personal vision would eventually come to pass. It never did—probably because that particular divine promise involved the imminent judgment of Judah some six centuries before Christ, not athletic evangelism in the twentieth century. This Habakkuk passage is not a *promise to us,* but it does yield a *principle for us:* God will do what he says. It is imperative that we look carefully at the context of any so-called promise and compare it to other passages of Scripture before claiming it for our own.

Third, even when we are convinced a promise or passage applies to our modern-day situation, our attitude must be one of submission to the sovereign plan of God. Our Lord has a divine timetable to which we are not privy. His will for our lives is sometimes inscrutable. He is working for our eternal good, not just our temporal good. Forgetting these truths and having wrong expectations may cause us to completely miss occasions when God quietly makes good on his promises to us. This is a critical point. Recognize the huge difference between (1) grappling with the character and will of God and humbly trusting him to do what he says and (2) the popular "name it and claim it" mind-set that sometimes borders on arrogance and impatience: "I expect God to quickly give me what he has promised!"

When a noted Christian leader was in the late stages of terminal cancer, a friend reportedly chided him for not praying more boldly for healing. The old saint is said to have responded, "When in the presence of royalty, it seems uniquely unbecoming to demand anything."

I hope that you will read and ponder the following pages with a trusting heart and not a demanding will. And may God bless you as you do so.

PART 1

LOOKING AROUND: THE STRUGGLES WE FACE

King Solomon, the wisest man who ever lived, once observed, "Nothing under the sun is truly new" (Ecclesiastes 1:9). This maxim suggests, among other things, that the painful struggles we face are universal. Throughout history, humanity has wrestled with trials, confusion, anxiety, fear, weariness, and sorrow.

The thirty readings that follow introduce us to a wide assortment of biblical saints in a broad variety of troubles. These passages remind us that tough times are a fact of life in a world that has rejected God's rule. More significantly, they give hope by promising the help we need to complete the difficult journey of faith.

THE PROMISE
GOD IS BIGGER THAN OUR WORLDLY TROUBLES

Here on earth you will have many trials and sorrows. But take
heart, because I have overcome the world.   John 16:33

HAVE you ever stopped to think how different life would be if
we were still living in Eden? No weeds. No difficult pregnancies.
No squabbles with spouses. No financial woes. No cancer. No
feeling far away from God. And that list doesn't even begin to
scratch the surface!

Instead, we live in a world marred by the effects of sin. We
daily face all kinds of pain and trouble—suffering, weeping, loss,
and despair.

The temptation is to blame our woes on God, but let's be
honest: The human race did this to itself. All God ever did was
love us and, when we rebelled, implement a plan to rescue us.

The promise above, a statement by Jesus to his followers, is a
sobering assessment of the way things are. But it is also a hope-
ful reminder of the once and future paradise for which we were
created.

In the light of this truth, author Elisabeth Elliot counsels us,
"Refuse self-pity. Refuse it absolutely. It is a deadly thing with
power to destroy you. Turn your thoughts to Christ, who has
already carried your griefs and sorrows."

PRAYING GOD'S PROMISE

Trials and sorrows are a normal part of life. I don't like this truth, God, but it reminds me of my need for you. I can take heart in the fact that you will have the final word. I praise you because you are powerful and sovereign over the events of life—even the hard times. Keep me looking to you.

GOD'S PROMISE TO YOU

- Trials and sorrows are part of living in a fallen world.
- Christ is bigger and more powerful than any worldly troubles you face.

THE PROMISE
GOD ALLOWS YOU TO GO THROUGH
HARD TIMES

If we are to share his glory, we must also share his suffering.
Romans 8:17

How many rousing sermons or best-selling books about the glory of suffering have you heard or read in the last year?

Despite the fact that the Bible speaks in great detail about the certainty of suffering and the undeniable blessing to be found in it, we treat the idea of suffering as we would our crazy, embarrassing Uncle Louie. We pretend it doesn't exist. We don't discuss it. We rarely make even the slightest attempt to see God's purposes in it.

The apostle Paul, a man well acquainted with suffering, said in his magnum opus, the Epistle to the Romans, that we should *embrace* suffering. Not only does it lead to eventual glory, as we see in the promise above, but God uses it to transform us here and now (Romans 8:28-29).

Henri Nouwen put it this way: "Your life is not going to be easy, and it should not be easy. It ought to be hard. It ought to be radical; it ought to be restless; it ought to lead you to places you'd rather not go."

Realize that you'll never draw a big crowd advocating such a notion, but you will draw near to Jesus.

PRAYING GOD'S PROMISE

Sharing your glory—how wonderful to contemplate that, Lord. One day I will be with you. I will see you as you are. I will share in the eternal inheritance that you have promised all your children. Your promise, however, is that believers must share the sufferings of Christ. Father, we seldom "claim" this promise. Suffering is confusing, painful, and something I avoid rather than embrace. Teach me to respond to the difficulties in my life in a godly fashion, and use them to transform me into the person you want me to be.

GOD'S PROMISE TO YOU

- Now you must share in Christ's suffering.
- One day you will share in Christ's glory.

THE PROMISE
GOD DOES NOT RESPOND TO THOSE WHO ARE REBELLIOUS

If I had not confessed the sin in my heart, my Lord would not have listened. But God did listen! He paid attention to my prayer.

Psalm 66:18-19

IT is bad to be in trouble. It is worse to be in trouble and on the outs with God. According to the passage above, penned by King David, if we are harboring sinful attitudes in our hearts or willfully indulging in sinful activities, we should not expect God to respond to our prayers.

This is not because God doesn't love us. He does—more than we realize. It's not because God doesn't want to help us. He longs to deliver us. It's simply that a holy God cannot wink at sin or look the other way. Intimacy with God requires honesty, humility, purity.

For us to attempt to approach God without first addressing the ways in which we have knowingly offended and wronged him is an exercise in futility. Sin is the "elephant in the room" that must be acknowledged and dealt with. Once we do that, we again enjoy sweet fellowship with God. Clean and forgiven, we can be sure he hears our pleas for help.

PRAYING GOD'S PROMISE

Lord, you do not listen to my prayers when I have unconfessed sin in my life. By your Spirit give me the humility I need to take a hard look at my soul. Show me, God, any wrong attitudes and actions that I need to acknowledge. I do not want to short-circuit your power and effectiveness. I want to be right with you. I want to be close to you. Thank you for pledging to hear those who humble themselves and acknowledge their sin. May my sins, which block me from you when I don't confess them, become a bridge to you as I admit them, forsake them, and experience your forgiveness.

GOD'S PROMISE TO YOU

- God does not respond to the prayers of those who have unconfessed sin in their lives.

THE PROMISE
GOD IS TRIUMPHANT OVER DEATH

Jesus told her, "I am the resurrection and the life. Those who believe in me, even though they die like everyone else, will live again."   John 11:25

WE will not speak here of the *fear* of death—the terrible uncertainty that so many feel at the thought of caskets and funeral homes and "the Hereafter."

We will not try to describe the *sadness* of death. What words can convey the incalculable sorrow someone feels at the loss of a loved one?

Instead, we will simply ponder the words of Jesus printed above. We will picture Christ standing in a Jewish graveyard, speaking to the weeping friends and family members of a man named Lazarus. There Jesus is—can you see him?—declaring in a clear and calm voice his absolute power and authority over death. Specifically, he gives assurance to all who trust him that death is *not* the end.

Whatever else you think or feel about death today, please embrace that truth. And in your times of grief, remember the insightful observation of Henry Ward Beecher: "God washes the eyes by tears until they can behold the invisible land where tears shall come no more."

PRAYING GOD'S PROMISE

Lord Jesus, you are the resurrection and the life. By coming out of the tomb, you conquered death. The grave has no power over you or your followers. Keep me from grieving as those who have no eternal hope. Those who believe in you will live forever. The old saying is true: "Born once, die twice; born twice, die once." I praise you for triumphing over the grave. I do not have to live in fear!

GOD'S PROMISE TO YOU

- Those who believe in Christ do not have to fear death.

THE PROMISE
GOD'S WORD ENCOURAGES THOSE WHO GRIEVE

I weep with grief; encourage me by your word.   Psalm 119:28

T HERE are so many reasons and occasions for grief. You may be grieving the death of a loved one, mourning the end of a marriage, or coming to terms with the fact that a deep-seated dream will never materialize.

In short, grief is about loss. It's the painful anger and emptiness we feel when we have to say good-bye. It's the sharp, soul-shaking sadness that never fully goes away. We don't ever "get over" our grief; we only learn not to be incapacitated by life's losses.

When Christians face deep grief, the last thing in the world many of them feel like doing is reading the Bible. God's truth, like strong medicine, can initially sting a wounded heart filled with pain. But applied faithfully, the Scriptures prove to be a soothing balm. God's Word does its healing work by bringing us back again and again to what is really true. In the words of author George Macdonald, "How often we look upon God as our last and feeblest resource. We go to him because we have nowhere else to go. And then we learn that the storms of life have driven us, not upon the rocks, but into the desired haven."

PRAYING GOD'S PROMISE

There is no escaping grief in this life. Thank you, Lord, for understanding. Your Word says that you are a "man of sorrows, acquainted with bitterest grief." When I am overcome with sadness and loss, encourage me as I read your Word. When I do not feel like hearing your Word, give me the discipline to come to you and listen anyway. Comfort me with your truth.

GOD'S PROMISE TO YOU

- God's Word can encourage you in times of grief.

THE PROMISE
GOD TAKES CARE OF THE GODLY

Give your burdens to the Lord, and he will take care of you.
He will not permit the godly to slip and fall.   Psalm 55:22

W HAT image do you see when you think of the adjective
burdened? A weary-looking middle-aged couple slumped on a
couch in the corner of a nursing home lobby? A concerned
parent staring through the curtains late at night, wondering
about a rebellious seventeen-year-old? A feeble widow
trying—not too successfully—to maintain a big house and yard?

Burdens come in all varieties (and they come daily!), but the
promise above is wonderfully reassuring. Whenever you feel
weighed down, you can give your problems and worries to the
Lord. He will take care of you, because he cares for you (see
1 Peter 5:7). And though we sometimes wonder whether we can
endure long-term burdens, we have the divine pledge that God
will never let go of us. He won't let us fall.

The more we ponder this, the more we can say with Frederick
Faber, "Blessed is any weight, however overwhelming, which
God has been so good as to fasten with his own hands upon our
shoulders." Such burdens keep us humble. They keep us looking to God, calling out to him, trusting in him.

PRAYING GOD'S PROMISE

In my life, Lord, burdens seem to be "new every morning." But so is your faithfulness! You see my situation. You know my needs. If I give you my burdens, you promise to take care of them and me. There is no sense worrying about situations I cannot change. I trust you, Lord. I will cling to you and your promise today.

GOD'S PROMISE TO YOU

- When you give God your burdens, he will take care of you.
- He will not let you slip and fall.

THE PROMISE
GOD'S PRESENCE GIVES US COURAGE

I command you—be strong and courageous! Do not be afraid
or discouraged. For the Lord your God is with you wherever
you go.   Joshua 1:9

A T bedtime the five-year-old child is afraid. Maybe it's the dark.
More likely it's the fear of what might be lurking in the dark.
Mom replaces the night-light bulb and speaks countless words
of assurance, but still the child trembles. Not until Dad enters
the room and sits on the bed for several minutes does the child
peacefully drift off to sleep.

Some might quibble over the parental response in the
scenario just described, but none would argue that there is
something about a good and strong father's presence that gives
children a sense of security and peace.

This is the point of God's promise to Joshua in today's verse
as the nation of Israel stands poised to move into a strange land
filled with strong enemies.

This is the point of God's promises to you: "Be sure of this:
I am with you always, even to the end of the age" (Matthew 28:20)
and "I will never fail you. I will never forsake you" (Hebrews 13:5).
He's with you all the time, and he is in control.

Maybe Corrie ten Boom's analogy can help you: "When a
train goes through a tunnel and it gets dark, you don't throw

away the ticket and jump off. You sit still and trust the engineer."

PRAYING GOD'S PROMISE

Lord, you tell me to be strong and courageous, to not be afraid or discouraged. With all that I'm facing, such commands seem impossible. I feel the exact opposite of what you are calling me to be and do! You promise to be with me wherever I go. Help me believe this pledge, not just in my head but deep within my heart. Make this truth real to me in my time of trouble. Teach me to live by faith, not by how things feel or seem to be.

GOD'S PROMISE TO YOU

- You do not have to be afraid.
- You do not need to give in to discouragement.
- The Lord is with you wherever you go.

THE PROMISE
GOD'S CHILDREN ARE DESPISED BY THE WORLD

[Jesus said,] "When the world hates you, remember it hated me before it hated you. The world would love you if you belonged to it, but you don't. I chose you to come out of the world, and so it hates you."

John 15:18-19

T HERE'S an old Peanuts cartoon in which Charlie Brown is sharing with Linus his ambition to be rich. But, he finally adds, while he *does* want to have lots and lots of money, he also intends to be totally unaffected by his vast wealth. Linus, realizing the unlikelihood of attaining such a goal, can only shake his head and say, "Good luck!"

In a similar way many Christians want both the world's acceptance and God's approval. "I want to follow Christ," the reasoning goes, "but I don't want my unbelieving friends and neighbors to think I'm weird. I want to live out my faith in such a way that I don't create waves."

"Good luck!" Linus might say again.

The truth is, if we really align ourselves with Christ, we will be lightning rods for worldly scorn. A few God-fearing souls will love and respect us. But many others will despise us—or at least what we stand for.

We don't want to think about a biblical promise that tells us that others will hate us. But it's a promise nonetheless.

PRAYING GOD'S PROMISE

The world hated you, Lord, and so it will hate all who identify with you. Oh God, I don't like the thought of being despised and ridiculed. But I want to stand boldly for you. Keep me from being obnoxious. Make me gentle and winsome like Christ. When I am ostracized and criticized for my faith, help me to respond in love.

GOD'S PROMISE TO YOU

- The world will hate you if you walk closely with God.

THE PROMISE
GOD USES PROBLEMS TO SHAPE YOU

We can rejoice, too, when we run into problems and trials, for
we know that they are good for us—they help us learn to
endure.

Romans 5:3

TELL the truth. When you run into problems, what is your first
and most common response: complaining? crying? yelling?
denial? pouting? rejoicing?

Unless you're highly unusual (or slightly dishonest!) you
probably didn't answer "rejoicing." Let's face it—it isn't natural
to be joyful in the face of trials. But we can develop this character trait. According to the promise above, trials are good for us.
How so? In the same way that an excruciating exercise regimen
is good for us. We sweat and strain through painful and
unpleasant workouts, but over time, if we keep at it, we see big
changes in ourselves. We're stronger and healthier.

Eighteenth-century British statesman Edmund Burke noted:
"He that wrestles with us strengthens our nerves, and sharpens
our skill. Our antagonist is our helper."

Such an attitude is crucial. Viewing your troubles as a kind of
"spiritual exercise program" enables you to rejoice (Romans
8:28-29; James 1:2-4). God is using problems and trials in your
life to stretch you and strengthen your faith. Without these

"stretching exercises" you'd be just another flabby, out-of-shape Christian.

PRAYING GOD'S PROMISE
Problems and trials permeate my life, Lord. I don't have the difficulties many have, but it does seem to take all I've got to keep my head above water. You want me to rejoice in hard times— trusting that you are at work. Rejoicing isn't natural for me, Lord, so make it my supernatural response. Teach me to endure so that my faith will grow and get stronger.

GOD'S PROMISE TO YOU
- God allows us to go through trials so that we might grow.

THE PROMISE
GOD IS AWARE OF YOUR SORROW

You keep track of all my sorrows. You have collected all my
tears in your bottle. You have recorded each one in your book.

Psalm 56:8

S O M E T I M E S tears catch us off guard. Maybe the sight of your
old junior high school does it. Or perhaps you get choked up
standing on a beach at sunset or during the playing of the
national anthem at a Veterans Day celebration.

Most times, however, our tears are not surprising. We cry
because we're exhausted or stressed, frustrated or afraid. We feel
helpless and perhaps a tad hopeless. And one can keep such
powerful emotions in check for only so long.

Psalm 56 is a prayer of David during one of those bitter times
in his life when his enemies were hunting him physically and
assaulting him verbally. Weary and worried, he cried out—literally—to God.

Hot tears and raw emotions all came flowing out. But from
this dark time in his life we find the bright promise that God is
intimately aware of our sorrows and is keeping track of each
one.

We shouldn't be surprised. After all, if God has the very hairs
of our heads numbered (Luke 12:7), why not our tears as well?

PRAYING GOD'S PROMISE

You keep track of my sorrows, Lord. Thank you for loving me, for watching and caring about all the details of my life. You keep a record of my tears. When your children hurt, Father, you hurt. When we suffer for the truth, we can be sure that you see and take note of it for the coming day of reward.

GOD'S PROMISE TO YOU

- God keeps track of your sorrows.
- He sees all your disappointments and knows about all your pain.

THE PROMISE
GOD IS THINKING ABOUT YOU

As for me, I am poor and needy, but the Lord is thinking about me right now. You are my helper and my savior. Do not delay, O my God.   Psalm 40:17

SOMEONE has said that companionship doubles our pleasures and divides our troubles.

Have you experienced that truth in your own life? You can encounter a tough time, but as long as you're not alone, the situation is somehow tolerable. It's when no one else is around to see or care, when we feel alone and forgotten, that life's struggles become almost unendurable.

On one occasion David lamented: "Troubles surround me—too many to count! They pile up so high I can't see my way out. They are more numerous than the hairs on my head. I have lost all my courage" (Psalm 40:12).

Clearly this "man after God's own heart" was at an all-time low. But a few verses later in this same psalm we come across the truth that restored David's peace of mind in the midst of such a rotten time. It's the promise above—David's realization that he was not alone, that God had not forgotten him. He was comforted by the insight that he was continually on God's heart. That promise made all the difference for him. It can also make a difference in your life.

PRAYING GOD'S PROMISE

*I am always in your thoughts, Lord. Help me to remember that,
especially when I am in need. Thank you for that wonderfully
reassuring reminder that you never forget me. You are thinking of
me right now! You are my helper and savior. No other help will do.
No other salvation is sufficient. Thank you for the way that tough
times keep me looking to you.*

GOD'S PROMISE TO YOU

- God is thinking about you right now.
- The Lord is your helper and savior.

THE PROMISE
GOD DISCIPLINES HIS SINNING CHILDREN

When I refused to confess my sin, I was weak and miserable, and I groaned all day long. Day and night your hand of discipline was heavy on me. My strength evaporated like water in the summer heat.   Psalm 32:3-4

ALL good and wise parents discipline their children. The precise methods vary, but the goal is the same: to train them to choose right, healthy, God-honoring courses of action. Negative consequences are the primary disciplinary tool. When certain misbehaviors consistently meet with unpleasant or even painful results, children will eventually amend their actions.

God uses this same process with his children. Hebrews 12 explains this "divine discipline" procedure, and Psalm 32 gives us a real-life example. King David had sinned (presumably with Bathsheba). For a while David refused to acknowledge or turn from his sin. The result was God-induced misery and a loss of spiritual and likely even physical strength.

The great English clergyman Richard Hooker in his *Tractates and Sermons* noted, "Affliction is both a medicine if we sin, and a preservative that we sin not."

In light of such truth it is always smart in the midst of a tough time to ask God whether your affliction or trouble is a form of divine discipline. Sometimes our messes are self-made. In those cases a repentant heart is the first step out of trouble.

PRAYING GOD'S PROMISE

Your hand of discipline, God, lays heavy on believers who are in sin.
You correct your children not out of spite or anger but out of love
and concern. You want what is best for me. The consequences of
divine discipline are weakness and misery. This world gives me
enough fits without my adding to my pain by walking away from
you. Thank you for the security of knowing that your love is tough.
It will not let me go.

GOD'S PROMISE TO YOU

● God lovingly disciplines his children who refuse to confess their
  sins.

THE PROMISE
GOD STRENGTHENS THOSE WHO LOOK TO HIM

The Sovereign Lord, the Holy One of Israel, says, "Only in returning to me and waiting for me will you be saved. In quietness and confidence is your strength." Isaiah 30:15

IN 739 B.C. the Jewish nation of Judah was in a mess. Instead of trusting in the Lord during her tough times, the rebellious nation had called upon Egypt for help. God sent the prophet Isaiah to confront the Israelites, and his wasn't a very user-friendly message. Isaiah used scary words such as *destruction* and *calamity* and frightening phrases such as *humiliated and disgraced.* Many of his hearers dismissed him as an overly religious kook. But Isaiah spoke with heaven's authority, and his words and manner must have caused a few sleepless nights . . . at least for some.

The details vary, but the principles and promise are still valid today. In life's dark moments it is hard to remember—and even tougher to believe—the old adage that the bitterest cup with Christ is better than the sweetest cup without him. Yet if we are to experience all that God wants for us, we must turn to him—and cling to him—in quiet trust. If we ignore the Lord and trust instead in other people or other things, we do so at our own peril. Our tough times will only multiply. When you turn to the Lord in your tough times, you will find help and strength.

PRAYING GOD'S PROMISE

God, you are sovereign and holy. Forgive me for acting at times as though I am in charge of my own life. Forgive me for trusting in anyone or anything but you. Blessing and strength are mine only when I quietly trust in you. Give me the wisdom to see that a rich, full, satisfying life is possible only when I look to you and wait for you.

GOD'S PROMISE TO YOU

- If you return to God and wait for him, he will deliver you from trouble.
- You will find strength when you quietly trust God.

THE PROMISE
GOD OFFERS TO TAKE YOUR HEAVY LOAD

Jesus said, "Come to me, all of you who are weary and carry heavy burdens, and I will give you rest. Take my yoke upon you. Let me teach you, because I am humble and gentle, and you will find rest for your souls. For my yoke fits perfectly, and the burden I give you is light."   Matthew 11:28-30

BETWEEN 1861 and 1865, U.S. President Abraham Lincoln is reported to have said, "I am the tiredest man on earth." Photographs from the period bear this out—they show a careworn president clearly haunted by the horror of a nation at war. Like most world leaders, Lincoln aged visibly, almost overnight.

That's what stress does to a soul. Carry life's problems, trials, and worries for very long, and you'll feel, as we say in the Deep South, "bone tired," "chewed up and spit out," or "worn slap out." Such weariness can be spiritual, emotional, or physical. But in any and every case the effect is debilitating. Weary people feel as if they are carrying the world on their shoulders.

If you know this feeling, especially lately, the promise above from the lips of the gentle Christ is great news. He invites you to lay down your overwhelming burden in exchange for a lighter one that is more your size. The result is true rest.

PRAYING GOD'S PROMISE

Lord, you invite all those who are weary and worn-out to come to you for rest. You are humble and gentle. You care for me in a way no one else does. When I have nothing left, I need to seek you out. I want to trade my heavy burden for the lighter load that you offer. If I am exhausted, maybe it's because I'm not wearing your yoke. Show me how and where I am carrying burdens that you did not intend me to bear.

GOD'S PROMISE TO YOU

- God sees when you are weary and weighed down.
- He wants to help you.
- Christ will give your soul rest if you come to him.

THE PROMISE
GOD SETS YOU FREE FROM TERROR

I have heard the many rumors about me, and I am surrounded by terror. My enemies conspire against me, plotting to take my life. But I am trusting you, O Lord, saying, "You are my God!" My future is in your hands. Rescue me from those who hunt me down relentlessly.   Psalm 31:13-15

L o t s of days we feel some measure of "minor concern." Occasionally we experience "serious anxiety." Then there are those rare times when we are overcome by "outright panic." A 3:00 A.M. phone call, a heart-stopping lab result, an unexpected pink slip. In those terrifying moments it's as though the earth has given way beneath us and we're free-falling to certain doom.

If you've ever had a full-fledged panic attack, you know how David was feeling in Psalm 31. He was a man caught in the crosshairs of numerous enemies and rivals. Despite his deep faith, he wrestled with an ominous and imminent sense of dread. He found himself at the crisis point described so succinctly by Elisabeth Elliot: "Every experience of trial puts us to this test: 'Do you trust God or don't you?'"

Rather than giving in to wild thoughts and out-of-control emotions, David chose to trust in God's control over all things.

Which is truer of your life right now—terror or trust?

PRAYING GOD'S PROMISE

God, I could—if I chose to—make a career out of being terrified by potential trouble. It's a scary world out there. Bad things happen all the time. Remind me instead that I am perfectly safe in your hands. Nothing can touch me without your permission. You are my God, and you control my future. I praise you for being sovereign over all the earth—and over my life. I choose to trust you and not give in to the temptation to panic.

GOD'S PROMISE TO YOU

- The one true God is your God.
- Your future is in his hands.

THE PROMISE
GOD FORGIVES THOSE WHO ARE REPENTANT

You would not be pleased with sacrifices, or I would bring
them. If I brought you a burnt offering, you would not accept it.
The sacrifice you want is a broken spirit. A broken and repentant heart, O God, you will not despise.   Psalm 51:16-17

CRUISE down the highway of life for very long, and you will
eventually get broadsided by an eighteen-wheeler filled with
trouble. Such collisions are unavoidable—there's no way to
anticipate them and no time to get out of the way. This kind of
calamity happens without warning, even to the godly.

More commonly on our journey through life, however, we
experience mishaps caused by our own recklessness. These are
preventable disasters. If only we had been more careful. If only
we had chosen a different course of action. What do we do in
those situations when we have run off the road and crashed, so
to speak, because of sinful attitudes and foolish decisions?

The passage above describes a time in King David's life when
he ignored God's warning signs and drove straight into trouble.
The result was a tremendous "wreck" that killed two and
injured countless others (see 2 Samuel 11).

David eventually learned that the only real recovery from
such a life-altering crash comes via the road of humility and
repentance. No excuses or pledges will do—just the heartfelt

acknowledgment of wrong and the resolve to avoid such
reckless behavior in the future.

PRAYING GOD'S PROMISE

*When I sin, Lord, you do not want promises or extravagant
attempts at penance. You simply want me to wrestle with the
gravity of what I've done. You want my heart to be broken by the
fact that sin breaks your heart. You want me to see that sin ruins
lives. Forgive me . . . restore me . . . change me. I want to be a
person after your own heart. Give me a love for you that far exceeds
the attraction of any sinful pleasure.*

GOD'S PROMISE TO YOU

- God forgives those who are broken by their sin and turn away
  from it.

THE PROMISE
GOD IS CONCERNED ABOUT YOU

Give all your worries and cares to God, for he cares about what happens to you.

1 Peter 5:7

A few questions for those with a tendency to worry. Pause briefly and ponder each one:

- What situations are you most worried about right now? Why?
- Of the various situations currently prompting your anxiety, which can you personally change? Over which ones do you have absolutely no control?
- What are the inward and outward signs that something has you really concerned and nervous?
- List all the benefits of worrying. What are some of the drawbacks?
- Is worrying a sin? Why or why not? Put another way, how do you think God feels when his children get panicky and fretful?
- Why do some people seem almost immune to worry?
- When was the last time you truly felt at peace?

Instead of worrying, the promise above encourages us to roll our problems over onto the shoulders of God. He alone is big enough to deal with them. And not only is he strong—he's also kind. He pledges to care for us in perfect ways.

Why not transfer your troubles to the only One who can solve them . . . and ease your anxious heart?

PRAYING GOD'S PROMISE

God, you tell me in your Word to give all my worries and cares to you. Why do I stress out over situations I can't control? Oh me of little faith! I'm sorry, Lord. You are concerned about what happens to me. I don't have to frantically try to take care of myself and all my stressful situations. You promise to take care of them for me. Teach me to trust that you will make good on your pledge.

GOD'S PROMISE TO YOU

- God cares about what happens to you.

THE PROMISE
GOD MAKES YOU SECURE

Don't be afraid, for I am with you. Do not be dismayed,
for I am your God. I will strengthen you. I will help you.
I will uphold you with my victorious right hand.   Isaiah 41:10

QUESTION: Who among us never struggles with insecurity?
Answer: No one!

Insecurity is a universal phenomenon that paralyzes some
folks and sends others into a frantic scramble. Insecurity basically
means that we feel vulnerable. We can't truly relax because we are
fearful that something negative is about to happen to us and we
are dismayed (i.e., perplexed, or clueless) about how to respond.

In his classic book *Mere Christianity,* C. S. Lewis compared
situations like these to a dog on a walk whose leash has become
wrapped around a pole. The more the confused dog panics and
tries to go forward, the tighter the leash becomes. The dog's
owner, understanding better than the dog the way out of the
impasse, must take an action precisely opposite the dog's will.

The promise above is perfect for such confusing, insecure
moments of life. It eases our fear and diminishes our dismay by
reminding us that the living God is always with us (Matthew
28:20 and Hebrews 13:5) to lead us onward. Can we get more
secure than that? The One with all power and the ultimate
source of help assures his people of the strength and direction
they need in every situation.

Are you willing to stop struggling and trying to go your own way and let God lead you out of your jam? The extrication process may be unnerving, but if you rest fully in him, he'll get you where you need and want to be.

PRAYING GOD'S PROMISE

I do not have to be afraid or dismayed, God, because you are with me. Thank you for your strong presence that drives away my confusion and doubt. You offer perfect strength and help. Instead of trying to face and solve my dilemmas on my own, I look to you. Guide me through these uncertain times. Let me be victorious in you.

GOD'S PROMISE TO YOU

- God is with you.
- He is your God.
- He will strengthen you.
- He will help you and lift you up.

THE PROMISE
GOD REVEALS HIMSELF IN OUR GREAT TROUBLE

Do not be afraid, for I have ransomed you. I have called you by
name; you are mine. When you go through deep waters and
great trouble, I will be with you. When you go through rivers
of difficulty, you will not drown! When you walk through the
fire of oppression, you will not be burned up; the flames will
not consume you. For I am the Lord, your God, the Holy One
of Israel, your Savior. . . . you are precious to me. . . . and
I love you.   Isaiah 43:1-4

GOD sent the prophet Isaiah to his rebellious people to speak
stern words of judgment . . . and wonderful words of hope. The
Israelites, consigned to Babylonian captivity because of their sin
and unwillingness to repent, would need to be reminded of
God's continual love and care. In the midst of great trouble and
suffering, the people of God would need comfort and courage.

The words of this Old Testament prophecy echo through the
pages of the New Testament. God is always with us (Hebrews
13:5). He is our Savior (John 3:16). He loves us with an affection
that we cannot begin to fathom (Romans 8:35-39).

It is a monstrous misconception to believe that the people of
God will not endure great trouble. Christianity doesn't guarantee divine deliverance from problems, but it does promise divine
use for trouble. Adversity, it is said, is God's university. As

theologian Thomas Holdcroft observed, "It is likely that Peter, who was delivered from prison, learned less than Paul, who stayed there."

What deep waters, fiery trials, or prisons are you facing just now? Ask God to teach you through those tough times that you are precious to him and that he loves you and is with you!

PRAYING GOD'S PROMISE

Lord, you are always with me in times of great trouble. Thank you for your presence, protection, and peace. You are the one true God and the only One who can save. I have confidence and peace when I remember your faithfulness and love. I am precious and beloved in your sight. I don't understand why you love me, but I am so grateful. Thank you, Father.

GOD'S PROMISE TO YOU

- God is with you in times of trouble.
- He is your God and Savior.
- You are precious to him.
- He loves you!

THE PROMISE
GOD TAKES CARE OF THE LONELY

Father to the fatherless, defender of widows—this is God, whose dwelling is holy. God places the lonely in families; he sets the prisoners free and gives them joy. But for rebels, there is only famine and distress. Psalm 68:5-6

MANY people subconsciously believe the notion that God is partial to those in high places—the prominent and the powerful, the well-to-do and the popular. After all, aren't these the trendsetters and opinion shapers of a culture? Aren't these the ones who have the influence to move the masses?

Tucked away in this celebration song of King David, however, are two short verses that tell a different story. In this passage we find the startling promise that the God of the universe is concerned not with the rich and famous but with the poor and obscure.

Downtrodden people have a special place in the Lord's heart. When God sees lonely people, he swings into action, "placing them in families"—that is, providing them with opportunities for rewarding relationships.

If you are lonely today, rejoice in the Lord's care for you, and keep your eyes open for the surprising ways he wants to fill your emotional emptiness.

PRAYING GOD'S PROMISE

Lord God, you care deeply for those who are often forgotten. I praise you for your compassion, for your constant care and concern. You are not only aware of those who are needy, you are also at work in their lives. When I feel lonely, let me look to you to meet my needs. You are a faithful father, deliverer, and provider. You are the source of true joy.

GOD'S PROMISE TO YOU

- God is a father to the fatherless.
- He is a defender of widows.
- He provides for the needs of the lonely.

THE PROMISE
GOD STANDS UP FOR THE HELPLESS

Lord, who can compare with you? Who else rescues the weak and helpless from the strong? Who else protects the poor and needy from those who want to rob them?   Psalm 35:10

In an ideal world the most vulnerable members of society would be zealously protected by the strong.

In *our* world the weak and helpless, the poor and needy, are often neglected, or—worse—they are mistreated by those with power.

Perhaps you know firsthand about such oppression. Maybe you feel taken advantage of by a tyrannical boss or creditor, harmed by an unfair landlord, or abused by a confusing legal system that seems partial to the rich and powerful. Whatever your unique situation, this much is sure: There are few feelings worse than being at the mercy of the mighty.

Take comfort in the words of Psalm 35. There we find the story of a mistreated David who found refuge in the promise that God stands up and speaks up for those who are too weak to defend themselves.

In a strange sort of way, being helpless is a blessing. If we have "friends in high places" and "strings we can pull," we may not feel compelled to turn to God. It is those with no "connections" who usually realize that they have access to the highest Friend in the highest place.

PRAYING GOD'S PROMISE

Lord, no one cares for the weak and helpless like you do. I feel weak and confused. I don't know how to defend myself against those who are after me. Rescue me. I look to you and you alone. You protect those who are vulnerable. Come to my aid. Help me to respond in a godly fashion to those who want to take advantage of me. Keep me from bitterness. See me through this dark time.

GOD'S PROMISE TO YOU

- God protects the helpless from those who would take advantage of them.

THE PROMISE
GOD RESCUES YOU FROM THE EMOTIONAL DEPTHS

I waited patiently for the Lord to help me, and he turned to me and heard my cry. He lifted me out of the pit of despair, out of the mud and the mire. He set my feet on solid ground and steadied me as I walked along.   Psalm 40:1-2

ALL really good adventure movies have a "quicksand scene." Someone steps into a "pool" of this mysterious, mucky substance and begins to sink. The more the person struggles, the worse the situation becomes. In the end, victims survive or they don't, depending upon whether they are good guys or bad. But for the quicksand scene to be believable [*wink, wink*], any survivors will have to be *rescued*. Everyone knows you don't get out of such a mess on your own.

This is somewhat like the picture we see in Psalm 40. David reports the helplessness and hopelessness he felt in the midst of an unspecified trial. Despair *is* remarkably like being up to one's chest in quicksand. Struggling does no good and in fact, may only make our bad situation worse.

Our only escape from such despair is in calling out to God and waiting for him to rescue us. This makes for some dark moments, but if, like David, we can bring to mind what we know to be true of the Lord, we will survive to face the next adventure.

PRAYING GOD'S PROMISE

Lord, you see me and hear me when I have lost all hope. Remind me that I need to wait patiently for you to deliver me. You are the One who lifts me out of the pit of despair. Your truth is what calms my fears and restores my joy. Teach me to live by faith and not by my feelings.

GOD'S PROMISE TO YOU

- God hears your cry.
- He will deliver you from despair.
- He will give you stability.

THE PROMISE
GOD HEARS THE CRIES OF THE DESTITUTE

He will listen to the prayers of the destitute. He will not reject their pleas. Psalm 102:17

T o hear some people tell it, God wants all believers to be financially prosperous.

Such an idea sounds wonderful. Unfortunately it isn't *biblical* (not if you take into account *all* of God's Word), nor does it square with the experience of the godly down through the ages.

Read the Scriptures. Study church history. Saints *frequently* do without. Saints *often* suffer. Perhaps even you are suffering—perhaps even today.

Psalm 102 is a moving meditation for believers in crisis. The historical background of this psalm is unknown. Some sort of enemy seemed to be approaching Jerusalem with evil intent. In this disturbing situation, the frightened and needy psalmist poured out his heart to God. Then he found comfort in remembering God's care and concern (see also Philippians 4:13).

One promise—the one above—sticks out. It is *not* a guarantee of riches, just the assurance that God hears and answers the prayers of his people when they are right on the edge. "Man's extremity," as Puritan theologian John Flavel wrote, "is God's opportunity."

PRAYING GOD'S PROMISE

Lord, you hear the prayers of those in financial crisis. I'm thankful that you know all about my current situation. Show me if I am being disciplined or if this is merely an opportunity to trust you and to grow in faith. You will not reject my pleas for help. You do not forsake your children. I am confident that you will supply all my needs. Show me what I need to do as I wait for you to act.

GOD'S PROMISE TO YOU

- God hears the prayers of the poor.
- He will give you what you need.

THE PROMISE
GOD HEARS YOUR PLEAS OF DISTRESS

Morning, noon, and night I plead aloud in my distress, and the Lord hears my voice.   Psalm 55:17

DISTRESS refers to the mental/emotional strain and/or physical danger resulting from a troubling situation. It can be mild—a motorist in distress—prompting uncertainty about the immediate future. Or it can be serious—a baby in distress, a ship in distress—suggesting great trouble, immediate danger and need.

In Psalm 55 we find David in deep distress of soul. His troubling situation has to do with a former ally and friend who has suddenly betrayed him and is now threatening his life. But David's unique circumstances are not as important as his response to those circumstances.

Notice his raw honesty as he continually cries out to God. Next, compare his initial desperation (vv. 1-15) with the confidence expressed in verses 16-23. What prompts such a "mood swing"?

That's easy. It's the assurance that God hears and responds to the distress signals of his children.

This is the mystery of prayer: We bring our troubles to God, and in most cases the first thing to change is not our situation but our perspective. If we know we have God's ear, and if we can glimpse things from his vantage point, we can endure stress without distress.

PRAYING GOD'S PROMISE

Lord, like David, I need to bring my distress to you. Forgive me for the times I pout or complain to others but do not bring my troubles to the One who can actually do something about them. You hear my desperate cries and come to my aid. Like a sensitive mother who can distinguish the various cries of her newborn, you can tell when I am really in need. Thank you for watching over me and bending low to hear my requests.

GOD'S PROMISE TO YOU

● God hears your prayers when you cry out in distress.

THE PROMISE
GOD DELIVERS THE FAITHFUL FROM SHAME

Those who look to him for help will be radiant with joy; no shadow of shame will darken their faces.　　　　Psalm 34:5

H A S this ever happened to you? You're in a tough spot, a real mess. But instead of looking to God and responding to your situation in faith, you panic. You end up making decisions that you later feel ashamed of.

First Samuel 21 records how David, while fleeing from the murderous King Saul, pretended to be insane when he encountered a Philistine king. Get the picture? This is Israel's greatest war hero and most faithful follower of God, but now in enemy territory he is depending on a man-made trick—rather than God—to save his skin!

Later, in reflecting on this incident in Psalm 34, David declares that God is faithful to deliver his people from shame. Could it be that David regretted his failure to demonstrate faith before the king of Gath? Could David be saying that when we come back to God after making choices we are ashamed of, we find the forgiveness and cleansing that puts our shame to flight? Could it be that this truth is just what you need today?

PRAYING GOD'S PROMISE

Lord, there is joy—not shame—for the troubled soul who looks to you in faith. When I am in trouble, keep me from the temptation to take matters into my own hands. Give me the courage to trust you rather than devise some kind of human scheme to avoid trouble. When I fail, keep me from wallowing in shame. Prompt me to turn back to you so that I might know your forgiveness and peace.

GOD'S PROMISE TO YOU

- Look to the Lord, and he will give you joy.
- He will not allow shame to touch you.

THE PROMISE
GOD'S WORD IS A STRESS RELIEVER

As pressure and stress bear down on me, I find joy
in your commands.   Psalm 119:143

S TRESS is what we feel when we feebly **STR**uggle against all the
pr**ESS**ures and demands of life.

Typically, stress comes from the sickening realization that
our resources are not enough. For instance, we have too many
bills and not enough money in the checking account. Or we
have four hours of work to do in ninety minutes. Or we've been
given a task we're not sure we have the skills to pull off.

Psalm 119 offers a little-known, seldom-used stress buster:
God's Word. According to the verse above, the Scriptures can
bring joy to children of God who are ready to pull out their
hair. How? By reminding us of what is true and giving us
perspective. When we keep our eyes on our all-powerful, eternal,
and faithful God, we realize that life's problems and annoy-
ances "are quite small and won't last very long" (2 Corinthians
4:17). Even though our resources are limited, God's are more
than enough for whatever we face.

PRAYING GOD'S PROMISE

Stress seems to bear down on me daily. Oh Lord, I'm afraid I don't always handle life's pressures too well. Keep me from whining and complaining. Show me how to find joy in your commands. What an example I would be if I were to live with joy in the midst of stressful times. Drive me to your Word, where I can find life-giving truth and supernatural joy.

GOD'S PROMISE TO YOU

● In stressful times, God's Word can bring you joy.

THE PROMISE
GOD HELPS THE BROKEN DOWN
AND WORN DOWN

The Lord helps the fallen and lifts up those bent beneath their
loads.   Psalm 145:14

T HE commercial was intended to sell some kind of medical
alert device. It featured an elderly actress lying helplessly on the
floor and crying out in desperation, "I've fallen, and I can't get
up!" Within weeks the ad had become a national parody, and
the woman's phrase was the punch line to a thousand jokes.

Real funny stuff, right? Only to those who have never taken a
tumble, physically or figuratively. Only to those who have never
experienced the fear of helplessness.

The world snickers at the unfortunate. But God? Never.
When he hears one of his children cry, "I've fallen, and I can't
get up!" or "I'm about to collapse under this crushing weight!"
notice what he does.

He "helps." He "lifts up." He can send such aid in a million
different ways. But he will never stand idly by, and he certainly
will never scoff at you in your time of need.

"Crises," author Catherine Marshall once wrote, "bring us
face-to-face with our inadequacy, and our inadequacy in turn
leads us to the inexhaustible sufficiency of God."

PRAYING GOD'S PROMISE

Lord, you promise to help the fallen. Sometimes I feel as if I spend most of my time on the ground, in trouble. Please come to my aid or my situation will never change. You lift up those who are bent beneath their loads. When I am weary and worn down, prompt me to look to you in faith. And make me sensitive to others who are heavy laden. Let me be your hands today to someone who has fallen and can't get up.

GOD'S PROMISE TO YOU

- God will help you when you fall.
- He will lift you up when you are worn-out.

THE PROMISE
GOD NEVER ABANDONS HIS SERVANTS

We are pressed on every side by troubles, but we are not
crushed and broken. We are perplexed, but we don't give up
and quit. We are hunted down, but God never abandons us. We
get knocked down, but we get up again and keep going.

2 Corinthians 4:8-9

THE town skeptic unexpectedly showed up at church one
Sunday. He listened attentively to a lively sermon from the
book of Acts about the many trials and troubles of first-century
believers. When the pastor gave an invitation for sinners to
come forward and give their lives to Christ, no one budged.

Finally, to everyone's surprise, the old agnostic rose from his
seat and walked slowly toward the altar. Taking the pastor's
hand, the man leaned forward and whispered loudly, "Reverend,
maybe more folks would consider joining your church if the
Lord weren't so rough on his most faithful followers!"

Do you ever feel like that? Shouldn't the children of God be
exempt from excessive trouble?

That's a nice thought, but it's not reality. The apostle Paul
understood as well as anyone that serving God invites opposition and pain and suffering. But notice what enabled him to
"keep going": the truth that "God never abandons us."

If you are feeling strong spiritual opposition today, let that
promise renew your resolve.

PRAYING GOD'S PROMISE

Lord, the forces of evil are intent on opposing me. Grant me the faith, courage, and perseverance to keep following hard after you. I want to keep going. I want to please you and have an eternal impact on those around me.

GOD'S PROMISE TO YOU

- God will not allow you to be crushed.
- He will never abandon you.
- He will give you the strength and courage to keep going.

THE PROMISE
GOD IS ON THE SIDE OF THE DESPERATE

Happy are those who have the God of Israel as their helper, whose hope is in the Lord their God. . . . He is the one who keeps every promise forever, who gives justice to the oppressed and food to the hungry. The Lord frees the prisoners. The Lord opens the eyes of the blind. The Lord lifts the burdens of those bent beneath their loads. The Lord loves the righteous. The Lord protects the foreigners among us. He cares for the orphans and widows, but he frustrates the plans of the wicked.

Psalm 146:5-9

W HEN life falls apart, if one can cling to the notions that God is good, all-powerful, and wise, then it is possible to believe that everything will (somehow and eventually) turn out okay.

Ah, but that's far easier said than done, isn't it? It takes rare courage, almost a kind of "spiritual stubbornness," to wait and watch for God to work. Faith is not a breezy, easy act. It does not feel "fun." Trusting God is alternately agonizing and terrifying.

So what are we to do in times of trial and crisis? Talking and praying with a mentor can help. So can attending church and worshiping in faith, journaling, opening up to a small group. God has provided a lot of different sources of help to get us through.

Perhaps the best prescription for a lagging faith is to practice solitude and try to listen to what God is saying. Take, for example, today's promise-filled passage. Such words can be life-giving to a desperate soul—maybe even yours.

PRAYING GOD'S PROMISE

Lord, you promise so much to those who look to you. Such assurances seem too good to be true. They seem almost mocking, for I am in trouble, and I can't find you. I can't see how you are working. Please help me. I cannot help myself. You are my only hope.

GOD'S PROMISE TO YOU

- God will help you in every crisis.

THE PROMISE
GOD USES TROUBLE TO BUILD CHARACTER

Dear brothers and sisters, whenever trouble comes your way, let it be an opportunity for joy. For when your faith is tested, your endurance has a chance to grow. So let it grow, for when your endurance is fully developed, you will be strong in character and ready for anything.   James 1:2-4

SOME Christians in the midst of trouble feel a strange obligation to pretend things are better than they are. Just watch and listen to their forced smiles, their overly rehearsed, tinny-sounding declarations of faith and praise. Clearly these folks are trying hard, but they appear to be playing—badly!—a role ("the mature Christian") rather than responding authentically.

Other believers react to friends and loved ones in crisis by bombarding them with Bible verses and Christian clichés. The intent may be to help those who are suffering to "get well soon," but in times of pain even true words can ring hollow and sometimes even have a stinging effect: "God is with me"—okay, I guess that's true, but I sure can't sense his presence right now. Why do I feel so alone?

The above passage from James suggests that trouble is a fact of life. It also declares God's goal that we develop depth of soul, not a superficial "Christian persona." In other words, it's okay to wrestle honestly and for long periods of time. In fact, that's the only path to a strong character.

PRAYING GOD'S PROMISE

Trouble and tests of faith . . . Oh Lord, that is the story of my life! Forgive me for the times I buy into the silly idea that you or others are impressed by plastic saints who mindlessly parrot Bible verses. You want me to endure and to grow strong in character. Make me attractive to others not because I wear a plastered-on smile but because I'm real. I want to be authentic as I grow in my faith.

GOD'S PROMISE TO YOU

- God allows you to go through trials so that you might develop a strong character.

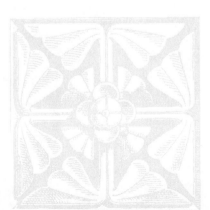

PART 2

LOOKING UP: THE GOD WE SERVE

A UTHOR A. W. Tozer wrote in *The Root of Righteousness,* "Satan's first attack upon the human race was his sly effort to destroy Eve's confidence in the kindness of God. From that day, men have had a false conception of God. Nothing twists and deforms the soul more than a low or unworthy conception of God."

These next thirty devotions are intended to help us develop a clearer, truer picture of God by pointing us to promises in which he explicitly reveals his character. Nothing puts our troubles in perspective like a glimpse of our majestic and merciful Creator.

THE PROMISE
GOD IS YOUR FATHER

> To all who believed him and accepted him, he gave the right to
> become children of God.   John 1:12

Most people in the world would agree with the statement that
"we are *all* God's children." It's a nice sentiment. It just isn't
what the Bible teaches. According to God's Word, unrepentant
sinners are actually God's *enemies* (see Romans 5:10 and
Colossians 1:21)! It's only when we put our trust in the Lord
Jesus Christ that we are reconciled to God and experience
forgiveness and adoption into God's forever family (Galatians
4:5; Ephesians 1:5).

For a Christian going through hard times, this "adoption"
truth is the best of all possible news. God is not just the powerful Creator or a righteous Lord, he is a *loving Father*. He sees your
trials. He listens to your pleas. He cares and protects and
supports. He is never harsh or impatient with you. He is never
"too busy" for you.

Take all the best qualities of all the best earthly dads you've
ever seen, add them together, and multiply by infinity. That's
the kind of heavenly Father God is to Christians who hurt.

PRAYING GOD'S PROMISE

Lord Jesus, I do believe in you. I have accepted you as my Savior and Lord. Thank you for revealing yourself to me. Thank you for saving me! Because of your grace and my faith, I am a child of the living God. I praise you. What a privilege! What joy to know that in every situation I have a loving, wise, and good heavenly Father to counsel and help me.

GOD'S PROMISE TO YOU

- You are God's child if you believe in his Son, Jesus.

THE PROMISE
GOD RESTORES THE HUMBLE IN SPIRIT

If we confess our sins to him, he is faithful and just to forgive us and to cleanse us from every wrong.   1 John 1:9

T HERE'S nothing like a tough time to reveal what we're made of. When trouble rears its ugly, scary head, either we trust the promises of God and respond with obedience, or we panic and react sinfully.

Too often we are guilty of the latter. When things fall apart, we become sarcastic, possessive, moody, self-centered, bitter, envious . . . or a hundred other unflattering things. Now the situation is *really* messy. Not only are we facing trouble, but we've complicated the matter by pulling away from God. Our doubt and disobedience have alienated us from the One we need most.

The good news is that intimacy with God can be restored by simply acknowledging our wrong attitudes and actions. The word *confession* in the New Testament literally means "to say the same thing." In other words, we agree with God—about our wrong choices, about his perfect forgiveness, and about the truth that we are brand-new people who have the power to say no to future temptation.

If you've added to your troubles recently by responding wrongly, confession is your bridge back to God.

PRAYING GOD'S PROMISE

God, I am often guilty of reacting wrongly in the midst of tough times. My faith is small. Help me to grow in you so that I do not fall apart spiritually at the first sign of trouble. You promise to forgive and cleanse me when I acknowledge my sins. You never move away from me. . . . I am the one who wanders off. Thank you for the fellowship I can enjoy with you by honestly admitting my wrong choices and claiming your cleansing.

GOD'S PROMISE TO YOU

- God is faithful and righteous.
- He will forgive and cleanse those who acknowledge their sins.

THE PROMISE
GOD DOESN'T ALWAYS ANSWER OUR WHY
QUESTIONS

There are secret things that belong to the Lord our God, but the revealed things belong to us and our descendants forever, so that we may obey these words of the law.   Deuteronomy 29:29

W HEN tragedy strikes, we are quick to look heavenward and ask why.

Perhaps this reaction reflects a deep-seated belief that God really *is* in control of all things. Or maybe in our grief and anger we're just looking for someone to blame.

Whatever the reason or reasons for our questioning, God apparently does not feel the least bit obligated to explain the cosmic purposes for our pain. C. S. Lewis, in his classic book *A Grief Observed*, reported that following the death of his wife, he knocked on heaven's door, so to speak, with deep, heartfelt prayers, only to hear the sounds of God bolting the lock from the inside. Then . . . silence. Nothing.

This kind of divine "no comment" seems to be a common experience for suffering believers. The fact is, you may never get satisfactory answers for why you are suffering. And even a detailed "press release" from heaven might not satisfy you. Head knowledge cannot soothe heart pain.

So what do we do? Realize that while God withholds certain secret information from us (Isaiah 55:9), he never withholds his comfort (Psalm 10:17).

PRAYING GOD'S PROMISE

Some truths are secret, Lord. Remind me that your ways are mysterious. I may never know the reasons for my trouble, but I must know your comfort. I don't necessarily need answers, but I do need you.

GOD'S PROMISE TO YOU

- Some things are not for you to know.
- God has revealed all you need in his Word.

THE PROMISE
GOD CALMS YOUR TROUBLED MIND

I am leaving you with a gift—peace of mind and heart. And the peace I give isn't like the peace the world gives. So don't be troubled or afraid. John 14:27

IN a fallen world what we have a lot of is trouble. What we have precious little of is peace. Peace of mind so that we can turn off all the nagging worries and what-ifs and find true rest. Peace of heart so that we are not forever paralyzed by crippling emotions. Peace of soul so that we can face the future with confidence.

Temporary distractions and short-term pleasures are the best this world can offer. These provide a brief respite from our concerns, but they do not fill our souls with peace. Though we escape our pain or medicate it, we still must eventually come back to reality. And there we are again: face-to-face with our external and internal storms.

What we really need is what Jesus offers: not the promise that we will have no trouble but the promise of peace in the midst of our tough times. Real peace. Otherworldly peace. Enduring peace. Peace is not the absence of trouble but the presence of Christ.

Who wouldn't want such a gift?

PRAYING GOD'S PROMISE

Lord Jesus, you promised your followers the gift of supernatural peace. I want so much not just to know about your peace but to really know it—up close and personal, firsthand. Your peace isn't like the peace the world offers. Keep me from chasing after counterfeits. I don't want worldly distractions or pleasurable diversions. I want the blessedness of resting in you.

GOD'S PROMISE TO YOU

- God offers you peace of mind and heart.
- His peace is totally different from the world's version of peace.

THE PROMISE
GOD DRIVES OUT OUR FEARS

God is our refuge and strength, always ready to help in times
of trouble. So we will not fear, even if earthquakes come and
the mountains crumble into the sea.   Psalm 46:1-2

THE next time you're at church or in a mall or at a sporting
event, look at the people all around you, and then consider this:
All of those people, no matter how "together" they may look on
the outside, are deeply afraid of something—losing a child,
losing their health, losing a job or a nest egg. And you? Admit it.
You have fears too. What is it that has the power to make you
sweat bullets? What is it *you* fear? Disease? Disasters? Death?

Psalm 46 is a hymn of trust sung by the ancient Israelites. It
gives us insight into overcoming our unique fears. There are no
simple steps to follow. The psalm simply reminds us of God. If
God really is who he says he is, we need never be cowering souls
who live in dread.

When a crisis looms in our path, our natural instinct is to
panic, but precisely the opposite response is called for. We need
to be silent (as in verse 10 of today's psalm) and focus on the
fact that God is God.

PRAYING GOD'S PROMISE

Oh God, you are my strong help in times of trouble. Forgive me for the times I act as though you don't exist. How foolish of me to forget that you are my security and refuge. I do not have to fear—no matter what I face. Teach me the holy habit of pulling back from troubles and focusing on you. I want to learn how to be still so that I can hear your calming voice in the midst of tough times.

GOD'S PROMISE TO YOU

- God is your refuge and strength.
- You don't have to fear because he is ready to help you in times of trouble.

THE PROMISE
GOD LOVES YOU IN TIMES OF DISTRESS

As for me, I will sing about your power. I will shout with joy each morning because of your unfailing love. For you have been my refuge, a place of safety in the day of distress. O my Strength, to you I sing praises, for you, O God, are my refuge, the God who shows me unfailing love.   Psalm 59:16-17

IT contains all the ingredients of a first-rate motion picture thriller: a delusional, jealous, paranoid king; a shadowy team of cold-blooded assassins; a young, innocent man running for his life. Only it's not just a fictional story; it's a slice of history from the life of King David. He is "exhibit A" of the biblical truth that godly people incur the wrath of the ungodly (2 Timothy 3:12).

In moments of great distress and crisis (and there are many recorded in the Psalms), David demonstrates three refreshing qualities. First, he always looks up, reminding us that in life's tough times, talking *about* God is not enough. We must talk *to* him. Second, he's always honest. He doesn't hide his feelings or mince words. He tells God all that is in his heart, both good and bad. Third, he clings desperately to what he knows about the character of God.

Read again the passage above. Better yet, go back and read all of Psalm 59. What truths about God can help in *your* tough time?

PRAYING GOD'S PROMISE

God, you are powerful. No matter what my trouble, remind me that you are greater and stronger. You are my refuge and place of safety. Thank you for demonstrating your unfailing love to me day after day. When situations are bleak and hope seems gone, give me the faith to cling to you and to look for your salvation.

GOD'S PROMISE TO YOU

- God is powerful.
- His love for you never fails.
- He is your refuge, your place of safety in distress.

THE PROMISE
GOD DIRECTS YOUR WAYS

I will guide you along the best pathway for your life. I will
advise you and watch over you.   Psalm 32:8

T HE first panel of an old cartoon is titled "Grim," and it depicts
a man falling from a high cliff. The second panel is labeled
"*Really* Grim," and it shows the same man about to plummet
into the open mouth of a hippopotamus at the base of the cliff.

Life is often like that, is it not? Sometimes our backs are to
the wall and our choices are "bad" or "worse," the frying pan or
the fire. What do we do? At other times we seem to have numerous options, but one is not obviously better than the rest. How
do we know which direction to go?

Answer: We trust in God's promise above to provide guidance and counsel.

Notice that the Lord doesn't just pledge to show us an "okay"
course of action. No, his Word speaks of "the best pathway" for
our lives. The overall picture here is one of concern. It's the
image of a wise and loving Father accompanying an unsteady
child on a long, hard journey. He is forever watching, directing,
leading.

Don't face your troubles—and don't make big decisions in
the midst of those troubles—alone! God wants to show you the
best way. Will you follow him?

PRAYING GOD'S PROMISE

You promise to guide me in the way that's best, Lord. Give me the sense—and sensitivity—to seek, to listen, to trust. You advise me and watch over my soul. I am so prone to wander off into dangerous places. Guard me. Keep me from a stubborn, independent spirit. Speak loudly enough that I can hear.

GOD'S PROMISE TO YOU

- God will guide you in the ways that are best.
- He will advise you and watch over you.

THE PROMISE
GOD KNOWS EVERYTHING ABOUT YOU

The Lord looks down from heaven and sees the whole human race. From his throne he observes all who live on the earth. He made their hearts, so he understands everything they do.

Psalm 33:13-15

T w o common experiences when we are going through difficulties are feeling somewhat invisible and feeling misunderstood. *No one really sees my struggle,* we think, *and even if they do happen to notice, they don't really know what it's like to be in this situation.*

That's true, except for one person: God.

According to today's promise, at every moment of every day God has his eye on each of the 6.1 billion (and counting) people of the earth. If that's not mind-boggling enough, he also knows what makes each person tick.

Theologians refer to this all-seeing, all-knowing attribute of God as his *omniscience.* Nothing about us or our situation is hidden from God. He has total insight into how we got to this place, what we're thinking, what our motives and desires are, why we do what we do, and what the future holds.

The verbs in the passage above speak volumes. Notice that God "looks down." He "sees." He "observes." And he "understands." He can understand because he made our hearts.

Pondering these truths won't make your troubles go away, but it will diminish your feelings of aloneness and remind you of God's presence with you.

PRAYING GOD'S PROMISE

God, you see me, and you know me. I feel alone and small and helpless. Thank you for the promise that you are always watching over me. You understand me and what I need to do. Oh Maker of my heart, give me insight into what I am doing and why, and what course I need to follow.

GOD'S PROMISE TO YOU

- God sees you and your situation.
- He made your heart and understands you.

THE PROMISE
GOD HELPS THOSE IN NEED

I am poor and needy; please hurry to my aid, O God. You are my helper and my savior; O Lord, do not delay!   Psalm 70:5

PEOPLE talk at length about the trials of Job, but how about the travails of David? Of the approximately seventy-five psalms attributed to David, a shockingly high number reveal a man in great trouble and turmoil.

Psalm 70 is a classic example. The specific circumstances in which David wrote it are not known, but clearly he was—once again—in desperate need of rescue from some powerful adversary. And so he cried out urgently, acknowledging God as "my helper."

In times of trouble, people with a superficial spirituality often lose their faith. Growing believers, on the other hand, use their faith, drawing even closer to the One who has words of eternal life (see John 6:68). David's example forces us to ask ourselves, "To what or to whom do *we* turn when times get tough?" Is prayer our first response, or is God our last resort?

As one who spent a lifetime being delivered by God, David would likely urge us, "It's only when you depend fully on the Lord that you truly experience his help."

PRAYING GOD'S PROMISE

I am in need of your aid, God. Hurry, Lord, before my troubles swallow me up. You are my helper and deliverer. No one and nothing else can save me. I depend on you and not on my own wisdom or strength.

GOD'S PROMISE TO YOU

- God is your helper.
- He is your savior.

THE PROMISE
GOD LISTENS TO YOU

The Lord hears his people when they call to him for help. He
rescues them from all their troubles.   Psalm 34:17

H A V E you ever worked up the courage to share a struggle with
someone only to realize that the person wasn't even listening?
Perhaps you got interrupted while talking about your problem.
Then, when the conversation resumed, your friend said something like, "Now, what were we discussing?" or worse,
completely changed the subject.

Ouch! Times like that make us feel as if our problems don't
even matter. Unfortunately, such scenarios happen often
because listening is a skill few ever learn and even fewer practice.
Even the best "professional listeners"—pastors and counselors—have moments when they have a hard time focusing.

Not God. The testimony of the psalmist above is that God is
always alert to the prayers of his children. He bends low to hear
our petitions. Imagine that—the Creator and Sustainer of the
universe "bothering" to pay attention to your prayers and even
the deep, silent cries of your heart.

With that assurance, take a long walk, find a quiet place, and
pour out your heart . . . to the ultimate Listener.

PRAYING GOD'S PROMISE

Thank you, Lord, for hearing me when I cry for help. What a blessing to know that I have access to you, that you listen intently to the deepest cries of my heart, twenty-four hours a day, seven days a week. Not only do you listen, but you pledge to rescue me from all my troubles. I need you, Lord. I look to you to be my deliverer in every confusing and frightening situation.

GOD'S PROMISE TO YOU

- God hears you when you call.
- God rescues you from trouble.

THE PROMISE
GOD IS ALWAYS WITH YOU

> Be sure of this: I am with you always, even to the end of
> the age.   Matthew 28:20

IF we humans could write the script for life's tough times, first
of all, there wouldn't be so many. Second, we would opt for
more happy, feel-good endings: more diseases cured, more
marriages saved, more kids off drugs, etc. Third, in our version
of things God would be front and center, rending the heavens
and making dramatic, just-in-the-nick-of-time appearances.
We'd have him speaking audibly, perhaps even holding daily
briefings with lots of Q & A. He would tour disaster areas,
giving out lots of hugs.

As it is, in times of trial God remains invisible. He speaks in
silent whispers through the pages of an ancient book. He desig-
nates proxies to do all his hugging.

His ways frustrate us, but they do not change the truth (written above) that he sticks by us when we hurt. He says he is with
you. Do you have the faith to take him at his word?

PRAYING GOD'S PROMISE

Lord Jesus, you promised your followers you would be with them always. I wish I could see you or touch you or hear you. But even if I can't, I trust your Word. This is not just wishful thinking; it's something you said we can "be sure of." I can count on you. Your promise is reliable in a world where most promises are not. Blessed are those who have not seen and yet believe.

GOD'S PROMISE TO YOU

- God is with you.
- He will always be with you.
- You can be sure of this!

THE PROMISE
GOD HAS SAVED YOU FROM ETERNAL DEATH

Having chosen [his people], he called them to come to him. And he gave them right standing with himself, and he promised them his glory.

Romans 8:30

WHATEVER storm clouds are in your life right now, there was a time when you were facing an even greater crisis: You were an enemy of God (Romans 5:10). Spiritually speaking, you were on death row, having been justly convicted of high crimes against the King of the universe (Romans 6:23). But God did a shocking thing. He put his one and only Son to death in your place. Jesus took your punishment and then, perfect justice satisfied, offered you a full, eternal pardon. More than that, God even offered to adopt you into his family so that you could share all his riches.

The point is this: If God willingly helped us out of the ultimate nightmarish predicament, does it make sense that he would allow lesser troubles to destroy us? Or as Paul put it just a couple of sentences after the verse above, "Since God did not spare even his own Son but gave him up for us all, won't God, who gave us Christ, also give us everything else?" (v. 32).

PRAYING GOD'S PROMISE

Lord, you have chosen me and called me to yourself. I do not understand such love, such grace, but I praise you. Thank you for saving me from sin. "Right standing" is a gift. Help me to remember that I cannot earn your approval. You declare me righteous solely because of what Christ did on my behalf. If you cared enough to rescue me from eternal dangers, surely you care enough to see me through temporary trials.

GOD'S PROMISE TO YOU

- God chose you.
- He gave you right standing with himself.
- He will give you his glory.

THE PROMISE
GOD IS CONCERNED ABOUT YOU

I no longer call you servants, because a master doesn't confide
in his servants. Now you are my friends, since I have told you
everything the Father told me.   John 15:15

T H E Old Testament book known as Proverbs is essentially a
divinely inspired king's best and most practical wisdom for
everyday life. Here's what the book says about friendship:

- The godly give good advice to their friends. (Proverbs 12:26)
- A friend is always loyal, and a brother is born to help in time
  of need. (Proverbs 17:17)
- There are 'friends' who destroy each other, but a real friend
  sticks closer than a brother. (Proverbs 18:24)
- Wounds from a friend are better than many kisses from an
  enemy. (Proverbs 27:6)

In other words, a true friend is faithful. He or she will be
there, through thick and thin, to the very end. A true friend
cares. He or she wants the best for you and so will try to steer
you in good directions even if that means confronting you with
occasional tough love.

Now, ponder the implications of that ancient wisdom with
the promise above, the pledge that the Lord Jesus considers

us his friends. How does that alter your attitude in your current trouble?

PRAYING GOD'S PROMISE

Lord, you are everything the Bible says you are—Creator, Sustainer, Provider, Father, Judge, Savior, and King. I praise you for being the righteous ruler of the universe—and for making and saving me. But you are also my friend. This means I can count on you to stand by me in tough times. You will walk with me, advise me, and care for me.

GOD'S PROMISE TO YOU

- God is your friend.

THE PROMISE
GOD WILL NOT ALLOW EVIL TO OVERCOME YOU

The Lord keeps you from all evil and preserves your life.

Psalm 121:7

P SALM 121 is one of a collection of "songs of ascents" sung by Jewish pilgrims on their way to Jerusalem for one of Israel's great feasts. Basically it is a hymn of trust that God will watch over his people as they journey along potentially dangerous roads, up through the hills of Judea to the Holy City.

Does today's promise from this psalm amount to a guarantee that God's people will never encounter trouble? No. The awful truth is that even Christians get robbed and mugged, raped and murdered. Statistics indicate that more followers of Jesus were martyred for their faith in the twentieth century than in the previous nineteen centuries combined. Try as you might, you will not find any biblical evidence to suggest that believers are exempt from the ugly violence of a fallen world.

The comfort you can take from the promise above is essentially the same thing that Jesus said in Matthew 10:28: At worst, evil people "can only kill your body; they cannot touch your soul."

PRAYING GOD'S PROMISE

God, your assurance to your people is that you will keep them from all evil. Thank you for the knowledge that although evil may come, it has no ultimate power over me. In the words of another Bible promise, "The Spirit who lives in [me] is greater than the spirit who lives in the world." I believe that you will preserve my life as you have promised. I want to live with the confidence that I am safe in you. . . . I am in this world to do your will until you call me home. I want to trust, not worry.

GOD'S PROMISE TO YOU

- God will keep you from evil.
- He will preserve your life.

THE PROMISE
GOD INVITES YOU TO COME TO HIM FOR HELP

This High Priest of ours understands our weaknesses, for he
faced all of the same temptations we do, yet he did not sin. So
let us come boldly to the throne of our gracious God. There we
will receive his mercy, and we will find grace to help us when
we need it.   Hebrews 4:15-16

W HEN we are scrambling around during tough times, trying to
figure out what to do, our minds have a tendency to dream up
all sorts of unlikely scenarios. Money woes, for instance, might
prompt us to imagine an out-of-the-blue phone call from a
billionaire like Bill Gates who is offering to bail us out. Medical
problems can get us daydreaming about an invitation to come
for a consultation (free of charge, of course!) with the world's
foremost specialists at a place like the Mayo Clinic.

The bottom line is that what we want most in times of trouble
is understanding and help from someone with the knowledge,
experience, and power to deal effectively with our situation. This
is interesting when we consider the promise above.

Look what that passage says about the Lord. He offers
precisely what we want and need. He has seen it all. More
important, he controls it all, which means that we do not have
to sit around by the phone, waiting for calls that will likely
never come. Instead, we have only to call on him. We have
free-of-charge access to him all the time.

PRAYING GOD'S PROMISE

You understand me, Lord, and my situation. I praise you for being my perfect High Priest. You know my weaknesses, and you understand the temptations I face. You invite me into your presence. You are never too busy for me. You will give me all the mercy and grace I need, whenever I need it. Thank you for the total, unhindered access I have to you.

GOD'S PROMISE TO YOU

- God understands your weaknesses.
- He wants you to come boldly into his presence.
- He will give you mercy and grace in your time of need.

THE PROMISE
GOD IS GOOD

O Lord, you are so good, so ready to forgive, so full of unfailing love for all who ask your aid.   Psalm 86:5

T H E adjective *good* can have such a wide range of meanings.

Good water is water that is free of impurities. To say that someone has good intentions means that his or her motives are kind and benevolent. We call land good only if it is bountiful and fertile. A restaurant gets labeled good only if it is praiseworthy; that is, it provides excellent service, an enjoyable atmosphere, and tasty food. A good dentist is one who is both gentle and skilled. A good friend is an intimate who is faithful, thoughtful, and unselfish.

When the Bible speaks of God as good, it includes all of these nuances and more. The Lord abounds in purity and kindness. He is imminently praiseworthy. He is always gentle with us, always seeing to it that we have whatever is in our best interests.

When your life situation is bad, doesn't it make sense to seek the help of the One who is the very essence of good?

PRAYING GOD'S PROMISE

You are good, Lord. Teach me to trust completely in this most essential of truths. You are ready to forgive and help those who seek your face. Like the psalmist, I want to taste and see that you are good. All that I need and all that my soul desires I can find in you.

GOD'S PROMISE TO YOU

- God is good.
- He is ready to forgive.
- He is full of unfailing love for those who seek his help.

THE PROMISE
GOD IS IN CONTROL

Do not forget the things I have done throughout history. For I am God—I alone! I am God, and there is no one else like me. Only I can tell you what is going to happen even before it happens. Everything I plan will come to pass, for I do whatever I wish.   Isaiah 46:9-10

FOR those who like feeling "on top of things" (which is most people, most of the time), one of the worst things about going through a crisis is the helpless sense of being out of control. Unplanned, unhappy situations suddenly throw our lives into turmoil. With all our plans and routines out the window and with the calendar now a giant question mark, what choice do we have but to wait and see where all of it will lead?

Nothing can make such times pleasant, but two responses on our part can make them less *un*pleasant.

The first response is to abandon the popular but foolish myth that we are in control of anything. The second is to embrace the promise above that God *is* in firm control of all things.

Our troubles may lead us to feel, as one has described it, as though we are "free-falling in the darkness," but the truth is that the big and good hands of God are underneath us and will keep us from ultimate harm.

PRAYING GOD'S PROMISE

You are the God of human history, the Creator and Sustainer of life. Thank you for being in control of not only my life but also the whole world. You alone know the future and can orchestrate the events of my life. Keep me from foolishly believing that I am in control. Help me to trust that you know best and that you will always work for my good and for your glory.

GOD'S PROMISE TO YOU

- God is God.
- He is in charge of history.
- No one can thwart his plans.

THE PROMISE
GOD NEVER CHANGES

I am the Lord, and I do not change.   Malachi 3:6

In your current or most recent crisis, what is/was your most reliable source of security and help? Certainly not your emotions. They can be all over the map. Probably not your circumstances. They change by the hour. Maybe you've leaned hard on loving friends and family members only to see their strength wane and their availability diminish over time.

The Scriptures tell us and experience confirms that the only sure anchor in the storms of life is the constancy of God.

Theologians label this divine attribute God's *immutability,* a big word for the simple truth that God is unchanging. He is not moody or temperamental. His love and care for us do not waver. His eternal purposes do not change with time, nor can human choices foil them.

The implications of all this are that we can count on God always and forever. When everything else has been washed away, God—like an eternal rock—will still be there for us.

PRAYING GOD'S PROMISE

Oh Lord, you are God! Help me to rest in the truth that you are above all things. You never change; you are the same yesterday, today, and forever. When my life is like a whirlwind and I begin to lose my bearings, give me the wisdom to anchor myself to you.

GOD'S PROMISE TO YOU

- God is the Lord.
- He does not change.

THE PROMISE
GOD IS BIGGER THAN YOUR PROBLEMS

Great is the Lord! He is most worthy of praise! His greatness is beyond discovery! Let each generation tell its children of your mighty acts. I will meditate on your majestic, glorious splendor and your wonderful miracles.   Psalm 145:3-5

HAVE you ever heard this old saying: "Big God, little problems. Little God, *big problems*"? It's a simple reminder of the truth that our response during times of trouble is a direct reflection of our view of God.

English theologian Evelyn Underhill reminds us that problems are unavoidable: "The spiritual life is a stern choice. It is not a consoling retreat from the difficulties of existence, but an invitation to enter fully into that difficult existence . . . and bear the cost."

So, in the inevitable tough times of life, if we see God as he truly is—majestic, infinite, all-seeing, immanent, awesome, strong, and compassionate—we will be more inclined to rest and trust. If, on the other hand, we imagine God to be absent, distant, impotent, unaware, or indifferent, we will surely panic and fret.

What is your common response when difficulties come and things fall apart? Do you focus on the magnitude of your problems . . . or the magnificence of your God?

PRAYING GOD'S PROMISE

Lord, you are worthy of praise, far greater than I can even imagine. Forgive me for the times I have taken my eyes off you. You are worthy of my full attention and total trust. There is none like you! Teach me to better focus on your greatness and majesty so that I might have an eternal perspective in times of trial. Faith is simply believing that you are exactly the way the Scriptures say you are. Increase my faith, Lord!

GOD'S PROMISE TO YOU

- God is great and worthy of praise.
- He is majestic, glorious, and able to do miraculous things.

THE PROMISE
GOD IS ABLE TO DO ANYTHING

You are the God of miracles and wonders! You demonstrate your
awesome power among the nations.   Psalm 77:14

ALMIGHTY. *Invincible. Unstoppable. Supreme.* All great words to
describe the infinite power of the living God.

In Isaiah 43:13 the prophet records this authoritative claim
from the Lord: "From eternity to eternity I am God. No one can
oppose what I do. No one can reverse my actions." The psalmist
declares, "The Lord does whatever pleases him throughout all
heaven and earth, and on the seas and in their depths" (135:6).
Theologians like to refer to God's limitless strength as his
omnipotence, from the Latin words *omni,* meaning "all" and
potens, meaning "power." In short, God has "all power." Nothing
is beyond him or too difficult for him (Genesis 18:14; Jeremiah
32:17, 27).

People in trouble have every right to call upon God's
awesome power. It honors the Lord when we ask him for "God
sized" things. But a word of caution is in order: Don't think of
God's might as being displayed *only* when your problems are
dramatically taken away. Sometimes the greater miracle occurs
when you are able, because of God's sustaining strength, to
endure crushing troubles.

PRAYING GOD'S PROMISE

Lord, you are able to do miracles and to work wonders. Remind me daily of your limitless power. I serve the God who can do anything and everything. You demonstrate your infinite strength among the nations. Demonstrate that same might in my life today. If you choose not to deliver me from my trials, then give me the ability to hang on and to keep trusting you.

GOD'S PROMISE TO YOU

- God is the God of miracles and wonders.
- He possesses awesome power.

THE PROMISE
GOD IS TENDER TOWARD YOU

[The Sovereign Lord] will feed his flock like a shepherd. He will carry the lambs in his arms, holding them close to his heart. He will gently lead the mother sheep with their young.

Isaiah 40:11

SOME years ago a matronly college librarian put a sign on her desk offering free hugs to students. Initially the sign provoked only raised eyebrows. But before long, a few disheartened and lonely students began to take the librarian up on her offer. Soon the trickle became a stream, and it is said that during final-exam weeks there would often be a line of stressed-out students waiting for a brief bit of tender loving care.

In a sense that's what the promise above offers. The people of God are pictured as beloved lambs in the flock of the Lord. And he is shown to be thoughtful, caring, and gentle—a Good Shepherd who throws his arms around the faithful and pulls them to his chest.

Sometimes when everything in our lives is going south, a little TLC is all we need to make it through the day. Will you let the Sovereign Lord hold you close to his heart right now?

PRAYING GOD'S PROMISE

Shepherd of heaven, you faithfully feed and guide your flock. Thank you, Lord, for your protection and provision. You are gentle, and you hold me in your arms. What an amazing promise! When I am afraid or worried or tired, remind me that you desire to carry me with all tenderness.

GOD'S PROMISE TO YOU

- God will feed you and lead you.
- He will carry you in his arms.
- He will hold you close to his heart.

THE PROMISE
GOD TAKES CARE OF YOU

How kind the Lord is! How good he is! So merciful, this God
of ours!   Psalm 116:5

I T would be odd to write a book on God's promises for people
in tough times and not mention Psalm 116. The lyrics of this
ancient song describe a distressing, near-death episode using
dark words such as *terrors, trouble, sorrow, tears, stumbling, anxiety,*
and *bonds.*

Whatever the specific situation, clearly this was *not* a carefree
time in the psalmist's life. Nevertheless, his troubled soul found
encouragement and help in remembering God's kindness.
Literally, God was gracious to him. He showed favor and pity.

If you want a stunning picture of God's kindness to the
scared and hurting, read all nineteen verses of this remarkable
psalm. God is pictured as being absolutely attentive to the
prayers of his helpless children—he "bends down and listens"
(v. 2). He is protective and gentle to his people because they are
precious to him.

Test him and see. In the midst of your tough time, remember
God's past kindness. Ask him to show his favor again. Taste
God's goodness in your life, and you'll eventually be able to
move from problems to praise.

PRAYING GOD'S PROMISE

Bless you, God, for being kind and full of mercy. Thank you for not treating me as I deserve. You are good to your children, taking care of their every need. I praise you for being so gentle and loving. In dark times enable me to fix my mind on your proven track record of kindness.

GOD'S PROMISE TO YOU

- God is kind.
- He is good.
- He wants to show you mercy.

THE PROMISE
GOD IS UTTERLY DEPENDABLE

The Lord still waits for you to come to him so he can show you his love and compassion. For the Lord is a faithful God. Blessed are those who wait for him to help them.   Isaiah 30:18

THE word *faithful* means reliable.

Old Faithful, a famous geyser in Yellowstone National Park, erupts every hour. Millions flock to see this monument to trustworthiness. That old pickup truck with 193,000 miles that just won't quit? Dependability. You can count on it. It won't let you down.

There are faithful people too. A faithful woman is constant and unswerving. She does what she says she will do. A faithful husband honors his wedding vow to keep himself to his wife and "only to her, as long as they both shall live." A faithful friend will stand by you through thick and thin, no matter what.

And yet no earthly thing is 100 percent faithful. Even Old Faithful has been running a little late in recent years. Only God measures up to that perfect standard. He is our faithful God, who always keeps his promises (Deuteronomy 7:9; Psalm 71:22). The Lord is so devoted to us that Psalm 136—like a broken record—repeats the phrase *His faithful love endures forever* twenty-six times in twenty-six verses! Get the picture?

Whatever your trouble, God is there. He will not abandon you. Turn to him, and let him show you how reliable he is.

PRAYING GOD'S PROMISE
God, you are waiting to show me love and compassion. Why do I look elsewhere for help? You are the one true, faithful God. Give me the courage to wait on you. Strengthen my faith as I see your faithfulness in my life.

GOD'S PROMISE TO YOU
- God wants to show you his love and compassion.
- He is a faithful God.
- You will be blessed if you wait for his help.

THE PROMISE
GOD IS PERFECTLY FAIR

He is the Rock; his work is perfect. Everything he does is just and fair. He is a faithful God who does no wrong; how just and upright he is! Deuteronomy 32:4

LIFE surely doesn't seem very fair, does it? We all see people who passively ignore or actively despise God—and enjoy abundant health, wealth, advantage, and ease. And we know those who love and serve God with great passion—and live under a barrage of problems. How can this be? How do we reconcile the great injustice of the world with the claim that our Maker and Ruler is always just?

This is, of course, a theological can of worms. The short answer is that the fact that we don't seem to see ultimate, universal, perfect justice *right now* doesn't mean we never will.

One day heaven's court will convene, with almighty God presiding. Everything in human history will be up for review. God will examine all the facts and evidence for everything that has ever transpired. He will consider and judge every single motive. He will address wrong thoughts and actions. He will commend every honorable and obedient response to his commands.

Until that time, remember that God is perfectly just, even if life does not seem to be.

PRAYING GOD'S PROMISE

Sometimes, Lord, when I look around, I wonder why the wicked prosper and the righteous suffer. Help me to keep my eyes on you and on the truth of your Word. You are just and fair in all you do. You never do wrong. I praise you and trust you. One day you will make everything right. When I am suffering, keep me from complaining and doubting. Teach me to rely fully on your upright character.

GOD'S PROMISE TO YOU

- God is just and fair.
- He is the upright, faithful God who can do no wrong.

THE PROMISE
GOD SPEAKS TO THE TROUBLED

All Scripture is inspired by God and is useful to teach us what is true and to make us realize what is wrong in our lives. It straightens us out and teaches us to do what is right. It is God's way of preparing us in every way, fully equipped for every good thing God wants us to do.   2 Timothy 3:16-17

A lot of people view the Bible as nothing more than an anthology of strange, dusty, old stories compiled by the superstitious inhabitants of another time.

But notice what the Bible claims for itself in the passage above. It says it is "inspired" (literally, "God breathed") from beginning to end. In other words, it is revelation from the living God. It tells us what he is like. It also, like a mirror, shows us where we have gotten off track. Finally, it has the ability to prepare us to be "fully equipped" for life. (In the original language of the New Testament, this fascinating verb was used in nonbiblical works to describe the outfitting of a boat or wagon for a long journey).

When we factor in other verses that describe the Bible as being "full of living power" (Hebrews 4:12) and "a lamp" that shines light along the path of life (Psalm 119:105), we begin to realize the tremendous resource the Bible can be to those in trouble.

Are you letting God speak to you through his Word? Are you letting the Scriptures equip you for life in a world of trouble and hardship?

PRAYING GOD'S PROMISE

Lord, thank you for revealing yourself to the world through the Bible. Your Word is a trustworthy and useful guide for life. Teach and correct me. Prepare me spiritually for whatever the future holds. Make me hungry for your truth. Give me an unquenchable desire to hear your voice, and meet me, I pray, as I look into your Word.

GOD'S PROMISE TO YOU

- God's Word can teach you and help you.
- It can prepare you for good works.

THE PROMISE
GOD GIVES YOU SKILL FOR LIVING

The Lord grants wisdom! From his mouth come knowledge
and understanding. Proverbs 2:6

S UPPOSEDLY, humankind's knowledge is now doubling every
three or four years. Unfortunately, despite living in the information age, despite computers and the Internet, despite countless
studies, reams of research, and an ever-increasing emphasis on
education, large numbers of people continue to do really foolish things. Why?

The ancient Hebrews defined wisdom as "skill in living." To
their way of thinking, wisdom was much more than just knowing facts about a subject. It was, rather, the ability to understand and apply truth to real-life situations in a fashion that
honored God. This explains how someone with a high IQ and
two or three Ph.D.s can rightly be called a fool. He or she has
great knowledge about many subjects, but all of this information remains divorced from everyday life. It is "book smarts,"
not insight and understanding.

We all need "skill in living" every day. But we especially need
wisdom when we're going through tough times. A wrong decision or foolish reaction when we're in a mess can make our
troubles even worse.

Ask your wise heavenly Father to show you what's right and
best. He will do it (James 1:5).

PRAYING GOD'S PROMISE

You are wise, Lord. Remind me of the truth that much of what the world calls wisdom runs counter to your character and to what you call me to. You give wisdom and insight to those who seek your face. How often I lack deep understanding. Oh Lord, keep me from making bad decisions. Let me see my situation from your perspective.

GOD'S PROMISE TO YOU

- God gives us his wisdom.
- He is the source of knowledge and understanding.

THE PROMISE
GOD SUPPLIES ALL YOU NEED

May God bless you with his special favor and wonderful peace
as you come to know Jesus, our God and Lord, better and
better. As we know Jesus better, his divine power gives us
everything we need for living a godly life. He has called us to
receive his own glory and goodness!   2 Peter 1:2-3

YOU'RE going through a hard time. You feel abandoned and
anxious. You feel helpless, powerless, and clueless. You know
you need to do something . . . but what?

Most people in dire straits react in one of four ways. Some
embrace the philosophy of *hedonism*. That is, they try to escape
their problems using the pleasures of food, entertainment,
shopping, drugs, etc. Others give in to *pessimism* or *cynicism*.
They throw up their hands and become bitter, even fatalistic.
Still others pin their hopes on *humanism* (man-made strategies,
self-help books and tapes, and the counsel of others). A final
group commonly resorts to *supernaturalism,* seeking guidance
from mind readers, astrology, New Age techniques, etc.

The apostle Peter offers us a different prescription: pursuing
an ever-deeper relationship with Jesus. In Christ we find grace
and peace. The better you come to know him and the more you
experience his goodness, the more you'll understand that Jesus
provides all you need to live as you should.

PRAYING GOD'S PROMISE

God, you bless me with grace and peace as I come to know Jesus better and better. Open my eyes. I want to see Jesus. Teach me how to develop a more intimate relationship with you. Your divine power gives me all I need to live a life that pleases you. Deliver me from thinking that I can find life or help or peace outside of you. You have all the resources I'll ever need.

GOD'S PROMISE TO YOU

- God will bless you with favor and peace.
- He gives you everything you need for living a godly life.
- You will receive his glory and goodness.

THE PROMISE
GOD IS YOUR REFUGE

[The Lord] is my loving ally and my fortress, my tower
of safety, my deliverer. He stands before me as a shield,
and I take refuge in him.   Psalm 144:2

N o trip to Ireland would be complete without visiting at least
one castle or round tower. Many of these ancient stone struc-
tures feature secret hiding places accessible only by extremely
narrow staircases and tiny doorways. These rooms were
designed so that in times of enemy attack women and children
could scramble to safety. There was no way that big, armor-clad
invaders could fit through such small openings.

This is a wonderful picture of the kind of protection God
promises to provide to his children! Look again at the joyous
declaration of the psalmist above. The Lord surrounds us with
his love. He is our fortress and tower of safety who shields us
from ultimate harm. All we need to do is run to him and take
refuge.

Such assurances prompt us to say with the apostle Paul:
"What can we say about such wonderful things as these? If God
is for us, who can ever be against us?" (Romans 8:31).

PRAYING GOD'S PROMISE

Lord, you are my loving ally. Nothing can separate me from your love. I am your child. You are my invincible fortress, my strong tower of safety. I do believe this promise; help my unbelief! Give me an unwavering faith. You will shield me as I hide in you. I praise you for bringing me through trouble. I look to you as my sole deliverer.

GOD'S PROMISE TO YOU

- God is your loving ally.
- He is your fortress, your tower of safety.
- He will shield you when you take refuge in him.

THE PROMISE
GOD IS ON THE THRONE

The Lord is king! Let the nations tremble! He sits on his throne between the cherubim. Let the whole earth quake!   Psalm 99:1

IN the darkest moments of our worst times it is difficult not to give in to despair. Every direction we turn we see trouble brewing. Meanwhile, where is God? Does he see? Does he hear our cries? Does he care? Has he lost control? Why doesn't he *do* something?

If that is where you find yourself today, the truth in the promise above can make a real difference. God *is* on his throne; he reigns over the universe and rules over your life. No matter how bleak things seem from your vantage point, the fact remains that God *is* in charge.

It's interesting to read what happened when the curtains of heaven rolled back, so to speak, and gave the prophet Isaiah (in chapter 6) and the apostle John (in the book of Revelation) a glimpse of the Lord on his throne. The experience didn't deliver either man from a life packed with trouble. But the reminder that God reigns changed each of them forever.

PRAYING GOD'S PROMISE

You, oh Lord, are the king of the universe! I praise you. By faith I proclaim that you reign over all! You are on your throne, and everyone and everything is subject to you. When my faith is weak and I am tempted to despair, remind me that you are still in charge. Give me a fresh vision of your kingship over the whole world . . . and over my world.

GOD'S PROMISE TO YOU

- God is the king of the universe.
- He is ruling on his throne.

THE PROMISE
GOD TREATS YOU WITH TENDER MERCY

The Lord is like a father to his children, tender and compassionate to those who fear him.   Psalm 103:13

COMPASSION is *awareness*. It's a bighearted, other-centeredness that opens one's eyes to the needs of those who are hurting and enables one to feel their pain.

Compassion is *attitude*. It's a strong desire to reach out and alleviate the misery of others.

Compassion is *action*. It's a generous lifestyle of demonstrating tangible, tender concern to those who suffer.

We all know compassionate people. What would we do without them? But in moments of crisis, what we need *most* is a touch point with the source of all compassion—our loving heavenly Father. Perfect compassion is what the Lord offers us when we hurt. He will move heaven and earth to help us in our time of need.

Listen to the wise words of George S. Lauderdale: "In this life, the Lord allows His saints to enjoy many sweet blessings, but none are more precious than those which occur deep in the valleys of disappointment, pain and heartache, where He without fail draws near."

PRAYING GOD'S PROMISE

Lord, you are a father to your children—a perfect father. Thank you for being strong and gentle, holy and approachable, a holy God and a loving father. Your nature is tenderness and compassion. When your children hurt, you hurt. Your desire is to protect me and give joy. Oh Father, let me know your gentle concern as I draw near to you today.

GOD'S PROMISE TO YOU

- God is a father to you.
- He is tender and compassionate to those who revere him.

PART 3

LOOKING WITHIN: THE RESOURCES WE HAVE

W RITING to a group of Christians mired in trials and trouble, the apostle Peter stated: "As we know Jesus better, his divine power gives us everything we need for living a godly life. He has called us to receive his own glory and goodness! And by that same mighty power, he has given us all of his rich and wonderful promises" (2 Peter 1:3-4).

This section focuses on thirty of those stunning promises—life-changing things that God has done in us and for us. He has not abandoned us in our tough times. We are not ill-equipped. We have the assurance of his presence and his power, and that means that we can not only survive our difficulties but also thrive in the midst of them.

THE PROMISE
GOD HAS FUNDAMENTALLY CHANGED YOU

Those who become Christians become new persons. They are
not the same anymore, for the old life is gone. A new life has
begun!   2 Corinthians 5:17

BECOMING a Christian is not a decision to "add God" to our
existing lifestyle in the way one might attach a new room to an
old house. Nor is it an ambitious project in spiritual renova-
tion—trying to "update" our lives with a religious paint job or
by adding new, shiny features.

No. Becoming a Christian means that the Lord takes his
wrecking ball and demolishes our old life. He starts over with a
fresh set of plans and from the ground up begins to build something brand-new, something altogether different, something
spectacular. The implications of this truth are staggering. A
true follower of Jesus, from the moment he or she exercises
faith, is a totally different person, regardless of how he or she
feels. This spiritual change is revolutionary, essential, funda-
mental, and an undeniable fact.

When we're facing trouble, it helps to remember that we're
not the people we used to be. We have the capacity to respond
in new and God-honoring ways.

PRAYING GOD'S PROMISE

Lord, when I first trusted in you, I became a new person. Thank you for giving me a brand-new life, a rich life that will never end. I am not the person I was—the old me is gone. I praise you because I do not have to keep living the way I used to live. Because of you I have the capacity to change and grow into the image of Christ. Let others see a real difference in me today, especially as I deal with trials.

GOD'S PROMISE TO YOU

- In Christ, you are a brand-new person.
- You are not the person you were—your old life is gone.
- God has given you a new life.

THE PROMISE
GOD HAS MOVED INTO YOUR LIFE

[God] has identified us as his own by placing the Holy
Spirit in our hearts as the first installment of everything he
will give us.   2 Corinthians 1:22

SALVATION would have been fantastic even if God had "only"
canceled out our sins. We would have had ample reason for
praise if God had "merely" guaranteed to get us to heaven one
day. But God did so much more.

He not only granted full forgiveness and the staggering promise of eternity with him, but he also moved into our lives. That's
what the promise above says. The God of all creation lives within
us—right now! His Spirit indwells us, giving us the power to live
and witness as we should (Galatians 5:22-23; Acts 1:8).

Do you see the implications? We are never alone. We are not
weak. We have not been left without guidance. And it gets even
better. The Spirit's presence, the apostle Paul writes, is like a
down payment, assuring us of infinite future blessings.

When life goes haywire, understand that you don't have to
scramble around looking for God. He's with you. In fact, he's *in*
you.

So obviously, he's also *for* you.

PRAYING GOD'S PROMISE

Your Spirit, God, lives within me. Thank you for your powerful presence. I want to live a holy life so that you will feel at home in my heart. I want to yield to you. I want to follow your lead. Cause your power to flow through me today.

GOD'S PROMISE TO YOU

- God owns you.
- He has placed his Holy Spirit in your heart.

THE PROMISE
GOD HAS GIVEN YOU NEW LONGINGS

I advise you to live according to your new life in the Holy Spirit. Then you won't be doing what your sinful nature craves. . . . The Spirit gives us desires that are opposite from what the sinful nature desires.　　　　　　　　　　　　Galatians 5:16-17

HERE'S a statement no Christian can legitimately make: "I don't want to do what God says."

Such a declaration simply doesn't square with what God has told us. The fact is, when we put our faith in Christ and the Holy Spirit took up residence inside us, we were fundamentally changed. We were given new life, new standing with God, a new nature, and new desires—desires to please God, to obey him, to do and be what he has called us to do and be.

Do I want to worship God in the midst of difficulty? Yes! Whether I sense such a holy desire or not, the fact is, it is part of me. Do I feel like worshiping? Maybe not on the surface of my life, but worship is the deep longing of my redeemed heart. Such a desire must be in me because God is in me.

The goal of the walk of faith, then, is to live out the new longings that God has already planted deep within us. At no time is this more crucial than when we are going through difficulty.

PRAYING GOD'S PROMISE

As a Christian, Lord, I am indwelt by your Holy Spirit. Thank you for coming to live inside me. Teach me to make decisions based not on feelings but on the facts of your Word. Show me how to follow the leading of the Spirit. Continue to help me to understand the truth that you have filled me with God-honoring longings.

GOD'S PROMISE TO YOU

- God has given you his Spirit.
- As you listen to his counsel, you will live as you should.

THE PROMISE
GOD HAS GIVEN YOU A NEW IDENTITY

We are citizens of heaven, where the Lord Jesus Christ lives.
And we are eagerly waiting for him to return as our Savior.

Philippians 3:20

W HAT do Christians mean when they say, "This world is not my
home" or when they make statements such as, "I'm only passing
through"? What did the apostle Paul mean when he referred to
us as "citizens of heaven"?

In 42 B.C. the Macedonian city of Philippi became a Roman
colony. A few years later the emperor Octavian ordered thou-
sands of Italian people to relocate there. Though far from their
homeland, these expatriates enjoyed all the privileges of full
Roman citizenship.

The apostle Paul used this actual situation to help the
Philippian Christians understand that followers of Christ are
"foreigners and aliens" in this world (1 Peter 2:11). As members
of God's kingdom, our true home—that is, our citizenship—is in
heaven. We're here only temporarily and only by our Emperor's
orders.

When troubles and trials come upon us, we can endure and
even rejoice. Our stint in this strange and sometimes hostile
environment will not last forever. One day our service will be
complete, and we will be summoned home.

PRAYING GOD'S PROMISE

Lord, I praise you! Thank you for forgiving me and giving me eternal life! Keep me from thinking as a mere worldling thinks. Though this life is filled with trouble, I know I'm only passing through. Grant me an eternal mind-set so that I can endure the temporary difficulties that come my way.

GOD'S PROMISE TO YOU

- God has made you a citizen of heaven—this world is not your home!

THE PROMISE
GOD CHANGES YOU FROM THE INSIDE OUT

This is the new covenant I will make with my people on that day, says the Lord: I will put my laws in their hearts so they will understand them, and I will write them on their minds so they will obey them.   Hebrews 10:16

For most of Margie's life, even after she became a Christian, little problems caused her to come unglued. But not anymore. Why? What happened?

Nothing sudden or dramatic. Just a growing understanding of the Christian life. Formerly, Margie lived legalistically. That is, she tried desperately in her own strength to follow a lot of religious rules. But that lifestyle was oppressive, and her days were riddled with failure.

Margie turned the corner when she began to ponder the difference between God's old system of law and his new arrangement of grace (2 Corinthians 3). It dawned on her that when she trusted Jesus, the Spirit of God took up residence in her life, changing her fundamentally and forever (2 Corinthians 5:17). Now she understands that the spiritual life does not consist of trying to comply with a long list of external rules but of relying on the power of the indwelling Spirit and living out the new desires he has already put within her.

Now when problems come, Margie sees them and responds to them in a new and different way (Romans 12:2). She's living from the inside out.

PRAYING GOD'S PROMISE

Thank you, God, for the new covenant. The law showed me your holiness and my own sin, but it did not give me the power to change. It is the new covenant, with the promise of the indwelling Spirit, that enables me to think and act differently. Guide me according to the truth that you have written on my heart. I want to obey you. Make me willing to do your will today.

GOD'S PROMISE TO YOU

- God has given you a new heart and mind-set.
- He has changed your desires.

THE PROMISE
GOD WANTS YOU TO EXPERIENCE
ABUNDANT LIFE

My purpose is to give life in all its fullness.   John 10:10

Far too many believers in Christ are living what writer and university professor Dallas Willard has called "vampire Christianity." By that he means that they are preoccupied with the blood of Christ but not so much the life of Christ.

The fact is, Jesus did not come only to forgive our past misdeeds. And he didn't come just to offer us the future hope of heavenly glory. He came, as the promise above states, to give us life *now*. Life in all its fullness. A richer, deeper, more satisfying existence.

If Christianity is about only a pardon for sins and a ticket to heaven one day, that's wonderful news, but it's not much help when your life is unraveling right now. On the other hand, if knowing Christ brings meaning, clarity, purpose, and perspective—and according to Jesus it does—then even hard times can be profitable. They may not be fun, but they will be filled with experiences and encounters with the One who is life itself (John 14:6).

PRAYING GOD'S PROMISE

Jesus, your purpose in coming was to give me a full and meaningful life. Forgive me for the times I settle for a drab, ho-hum existence. Forgive me for being so preoccupied with the stuff of earth that I fail to seek you or even hear you. My faith isn't just about the past (my sins) or the future (heaven); it's about life now—walking with you, trusting you, clinging to you—and finding you faithful.

GOD'S PROMISE TO YOU

- God offers you a rich, satisfying life.

THE PROMISE
GOD HAS GIVEN YOU ALL YOU NEED IN CHRIST

In Christ the fullness of God lives in a human body, and you
are complete through your union with Christ.   Colossians 2:9-10

W HAT'S lacking in your life? A spouse? Children? A group of
friends (or for that matter, even *one* friend)? A church family? A
job? An extra $25,000 a year? A house or car? A college degree? A
retirement plan? A hobby? A solution to your most pressing
problem? The truth is, each of us could list some missing
things—good things—that, if acquired, would enhance our lives
and make us feel more complete.

Now, are you ready to have your categories flipped upside
down? According to the promise above, if you know Christ, you
already are complete. You've been given all you'll ever need.

Remember who Jesus is: God in human flesh, infinite,
perfect, lacking nothing.

Then remember that according to the New Testament, Christ
lives in you.

Now, think about the ramifications of these truths when you
are financially stretched, emotionally flat, or physically ill; when
a friendship is sour or the job isn't going so well; when the
atmosphere at home is tense. Allow your union with Christ to
make the difference. Lean on him for what you need. His
resources are without limit.

PRAYING GOD'S PROMISE

Lord Jesus, you are fully human and fully divine. What a mystery!
I praise you for becoming man and living among us. In coming,
you showed us what the Father is like. In dying, you offered us the
very life of God. I am complete through my union with Christ! By
grace, through faith, I am eternally linked to you. Thank you for
fully meeting all my needs. Forgive me for the times I foolishly look
to worldly things in an attempt to feel complete. I already am
complete—in you.

GOD'S PROMISE TO YOU

- Christ is fully God.
- You are one with Christ.
- You are complete in Christ.

THE PROMISE
GOD PRODUCES CHANGE IN AND THROUGH US

[Jesus said,] "Yes, I am the vine; you are the branches. Those who remain in me, and I in them, will produce much fruit. For apart from me you can do nothing."   John 15:5

ONE of the most appealing features of the gospel has to be the prospect of change. God replaces old, wrong attitudes and habits. He gives us new abilities and opportunities to make an impact. In short, God wants to work in us and through us.

The Bible, in describing this process of spiritual growth, often uses agricultural imagery. In the words of Christ, above, we read that as we mature in our faith, we will bear "fruit." But notice what Jesus says: We must "remain" in him. Separate a branch from its life-giving vine, and the branch not only ceases to bear fruit, it also withers and dies.

In verse 2 of this same passage Christ reveals that branches must be pruned to increase their production of fruit. This is an unsettling image and a painful thought, but the idea seems to be twofold: (1) there can be no growth or fruitfulness without pain, and (2) the Lord uses our troubles for his glory and our good. The next time the pain of "pruning" feels unbearable, ask God to help you to focus on the growth and fruitfulness Christ is producing in you.

PRAYING GOD'S PROMISE

Lord, you are the life-giving vine; I am just a branch. As long as I am firmly attached to you, I will grow and be healthy and bear fruit. Please change me. Use me. Apart from you, I can do nothing. Remind me that there is no life and no life change apart from you. Help me to cling to you when times are tough, knowing that faithfulness always leads to fruitfulness.

GOD'S PROMISE TO YOU

- You will bear fruit when you cling to Christ.

THE PROMISE
GOD GIVES US THE ABILITY TO LOVE

When the Holy Spirit controls our lives, he will produce this kind of fruit in us: love.   Galatians 5:22

W HEN troubles come, our instinctive reaction is to "circle the wagons" and turn inward. Forget the destination, forget other people. Our top priority has just become survival. It's every man for himself.

That's our *natural* tendency. And yet God calls his children to an *unnatural* response: to look out for and love others even when we are hurting.

This strikes us as impossible, doesn't it? And it would be, of course, except for the Spirit of God, who lives inside us. The presence of the Spirit means that God's infinite love is readily available to us. By allowing his love and compassion to flow through us, we can make a difference in the lives of others even when we are beset by problems. What is the lesson here? Selfishness is natural. Selflessness is supernatural.

In other words, when tough times come, you don't have to circle the wagons. Keep moving forward. Keep caring for others. You don't have to look out for number one. God will protect and provide for you.

PRAYING GOD'S PROMISE

Your Spirit lives in me, God. I praise you for the presence of the Counselor, the Comforter, the One who leads into truth and convicts of sin. It is only by the Spirit that I am able to love others as I should. Spirit of God, do not merely live in me—control me! Change me! Fill me! I do not want to be self-centered. I want to be marked by your love for others.

GOD'S PROMISE TO YOU

- When you are filled with God's Spirit, he will fill you with supernatural love.

THE PROMISE
GOD GIVES US SUPERNATURAL JOY

> When the Holy Spirit controls our lives, he will produce this
> kind of fruit in us: . . . joy.   Galatians 5:22

IF it's short-term pleasure or laughter you want, well then, you can almost certainly find it, and God need not be involved. Entertainment, comfort, luxury—these experiences are readily available in our culture. (Just be sure to bring your credit card!) Happiness is a bit more tricky—circumstances have to fall into place just so—but happiness is also findable, at least for brief periods.

Then there's the rare jewel of joy. Joy is the quiet delight that comes from knowing one is right with God. It is a deep pleasure of soul that comes from living consciously in God's presence (Psalm 16:11). Joy isn't giddiness or feeling tingly; it is more an abiding radiance and elation that fill us when we give the Spirit of God total freedom to work in us in whatever way he wants.

For many Christians—especially those in crisis—joy is the most elusive of fruits. But it need not be. The Spirit of God specializes in producing this quality in the people of God, often in spite of their difficult circumstances. Will you let him have his way in you today?

PRAYING GOD'S PROMISE

Holy Spirit of God, I need the joy that only you can give. Forgive me for the times I let circumstances control my moods. Let me know your presence today and the quiet thrill that comes from walking with you. I cannot manufacture this supernatural quality in my own heart. Shine in me and through me for your own glory.

GOD'S PROMISE TO YOU

- When God's Spirit reigns in your life, he will fill you with joy.

THE PROMISE
GOD GIVES HIS CHILDREN OVERFLOWING JOY

[Jesus said,] "I have loved you even as the Father has loved me. Remain in my love. When you obey me, you remain in my love, just as I obey my Father and remain in his love. I have told you this so that you will be filled with my joy. Yes, your joy will overflow!" John 15:9-11

W HY another devotional about joy?

Because of the "never say die" misconception in some quarters that the Christian life is, at best, a dreary existence and at worst, a grim process of spiritual survival.

No! Jesus wants our lives to be rich and full (John 10:10). The Bible demonstrates repeatedly that joy *can* be our companion—even during life's worst moments. William Vander Hoven has noted: "Life need not be easy to be joyful. Joy is not the absence of trouble but the presence of Christ." We've all known believers who understood that truth. Despite hard times they were filled to overflowing with joy. Tell the truth—is anything more eye-catching or more attractive than that?

Whatever your current difficulty, the more you are convinced of Christ's unconditional love for you, and the more you are committed to loving him in return by obeying all that he commands, the more you will know the supernatural joy of Jesus.

PRAYING GOD'S PROMISE

You want me to know your love, Lord. I demonstrate love and experience love as I obey you. Rekindle my desire to live as you command. You want me to overflow with joy. Make my eyes dance with joy. Despite my troubles, put a supernatural spring in my step. Fill my soul with delight as I seek you and obey you and taste your goodness. Make me attractive to those trapped in joyless lives.

GOD'S PROMISE TO YOU

- God loves you.
- You experience his love when you obey his will.
- His love results in great joy.

THE PROMISE
GOD GIVES US WONDERFUL PEACE

When the Holy Spirit controls our lives, he will produce this kind of fruit in us: . . . peace.
Galatians 5:22

T HE world is not terribly impressed with Christian T-shirts, billboards, and bumper stickers. In fact, truth be told, many unbelievers are *turned off* by these impersonal attempts at witnessing. However, the world is stunned when it sees a Christian overflowing with peace despite a personal crisis. "Her life is falling apart, but she isn't. How is that possible?" "If I were in his shoes, I'd be a nervous wreck, but he is so calm. Why?"

The peace that the Holy Spirit produces within us is supernatural tranquillity of soul. Storms can be raging all about us, but within us is the calm assurance that God has already saved us from our worst predicament—sin and death. Would he rescue us for the world to come only to turn around and abandon us in this world? Of course not!

The Spirit-filled Christian is peaceful because he or she knows the perfect love that drives away fear (1 John 4:18). Ask God to give you his peace in the midst of the storms you are experiencing.

PRAYING GOD'S PROMISE

I want to be marked by your peace, Lord. I need it so that I don't worry myself silly. More than that, I need it for your glory—so that others might see the wonderful comfort and assurance that is available only in you. Teach me how to rest in the knowledge that you are in control.

GOD'S PROMISE TO YOU

- When God's Spirit has free reign in your life, you will know his perfect peace.

THE PROMISE
GOD GIVES US SUPERNATURAL PATIENCE

> When the Holy Spirit controls our lives, he will produce this
> kind of fruit in us: . . . patience.   Galatians 5:22

WHY does it seem that trouble always rears its head just when
we start to make real progress? And why do so many difficulties
linger for what seems an eternity? Why are some people so
annoying? And what recourse do we have when we can't exactly
swap the irritating folks in our lives (family members, cowork-
ers, neighbors) for a more congenial bunch?

When we're in these kinds of situations, when we're feeling
stuck, restless, and unable to change anything, we need the
miracle of God's patience.

The patience the apostle Paul is speaking of in Galatians 5
means endurance, steadfastness, or perseverance. To use an
older word, patience is the quality of long-suffering; that is,
continuing to "hang in there" even when your difficulties seem
interminable.

The next time circumstances put you in an unpleasant "holding pattern," the next time an annoying person pushes your
buttons, relinquish control of the situation and your own
emotions and will to the One who has an endless supply of
patience.

The results really *are* miraculous.

PRAYING GOD'S PROMISE

I want to know your patience, Lord. Forgive me for getting so irritated at situations and people. I want to be even-keeled. I want to be a person who holds up under the strain of tough situations. I want to be willing to wait for you no matter how long it takes.

GOD'S PROMISE TO YOU

- Those controlled by God's Spirit will experience supernatural patience.

THE PROMISE
GOD SUPPLIES US WITH HIS KINDNESS
AND GOODNESS

When the Holy Spirit controls our lives, he will produce this kind of fruit in us: . . . kindness, goodness. Galatians 5:22

O N that ghastly Friday morning, which ironically has become known as "Good Friday," Jesus was a swollen, bloody mess. Most of his friends had hightailed it hours before, leaving him alone to face the physical agony of crucifixion, the emotional anguish of a jeering crowd, and the spiritual horror of separation from God the Father.

Yet during this entire nightmare, Christ responded, well, *strangely*. On the way to his execution, he paused to console a group of grief-stricken women. He used what little breath he was able to catch to pray for those who were so merciless to him. He demonstrated compassion and forgiveness to a criminal dying at his side. And he took pains, literally, to see that his grief-stricken mother below him would be cared for by a friend.

In the ultimate "tough time," Christ oozed kindness and goodness. And because his Spirit lives in us, we also have the capacity to use personal tragedy as an opportunity to care for others.

PRAYING GOD'S PROMISE

Cause your kindness and goodness to flow through me, Lord. It is not natural for me to think of others or to think of glorifying you, especially when my own life is filled with pain. Teach me to live supernaturally. I want to be selfless like you, Jesus, always looking for opportunities to bless others.

GOD'S PROMISE TO YOU

- Those controlled by God's Spirit will be marked by pure kindness and goodness.

THE PROMISE
GOD GIVES US THE ABILITY TO BE FAITHFUL

When the Holy Spirit controls our lives, he will produce this kind of fruit in us: . . . faithfulness.　　　　　Galatians 5:22

WHEN big problems come, there is something in all of us that wants to bail out, throw in the towel, wave the white flag of surrender, and retreat to someplace less stressful.

This explains why so many people under great stress and strain walk away from God, a marriage, a friendship, or a church. When the future looks stormy or uncertain, it becomes easy to rationalize, to jettison one's convictions, to go back on promises: "Look, I know I said I would _____, but I never anticipated *this* situation! Everything is different now."

Before you succumb to panic and start to renege on a commitment, you need to strongly consider the promise above. It tells us that we have something within us (Some*one,* actually) who desires for us to be loyal and who gives us the courage and grit to hang tough. The Holy Spirit will, if you ask him, enable you to persevere—even in the face of overwhelming trouble.

PRAYING GOD'S PROMISE

God, you are always faithful to me. By the power of your Spirit, help me to keep my commitments in tough times. I want to be reliable and trustworthy. I want to be wholly devoted to you, through thick and thin. Fill me with your Spirit so that I have the courage to stand firm.

GOD'S PROMISE TO YOU

- Those empowered by God's Spirit will exhibit God-honoring faithfulness.

THE PROMISE
GOD GIVES US THE CAPACITY TO BE GENTLE

When the Holy Spirit controls our lives, he will produce this kind of fruit in us: . . . gentleness.　　　　　Galatians 5:22-23

ARE you a *gentle* person?

What about when the pressure is on? As situations become unpleasant, are you able to maintain your composure? What about when you have to deal with those who are asking "dumb questions"? What about those times when a kid or a colleague has just pulled a really boneheaded stunt, one with irritating, time-consuming consequences? Are you gentle when responding to mean people, perhaps even to those who are attacking you harshly and unjustly?

Once again Galatians 5 shows us the remarkable difference in a person whose life is under the control and power of the Holy Spirit. Such a person is able to keep ugly emotions from taking over and spilling out. In a gentle soul there are no embarrassing outbursts of grouchiness or anger, no displays of withering sarcasm or irritability.

The person controlled by the Spirit is *never* mean-spirited or vengeful because the Spirit of God never is.

Would you like to experience the "supernatural strength under control" that the New Testament calls gentleness? Yield yourself fully to the Spirit of God, asking him to permeate your thoughts and dominate your will.

PRAYING GOD'S PROMISE

God, when life is sour and people are rude, I need your gentleness.
Forgive my sinful tendency to lash out, to flare, to complain bitterly,
to react harshly or meanly. Such behavior is dishonoring to you and
is unworthy of a child of God. Teach me how to exchange my
crankiness for your gentleness.

GOD'S PROMISE TO YOU

- Those filled with God's Spirit will be marked by gentleness.

THE PROMISE
GOD ENABLES US TO REFRAIN FROM
SINFUL DESIRES

When the Holy Spirit controls our lives, he will produce this kind of fruit in us: . . . self-control.   Galatians 5:22-23

PERHAPS the dominant emotion in times of deep struggle or crisis is feeling out-of-control. Life has taken you down a road you never anticipated and you would rather not be on. You're experiencing unpleasant emotions you would rather not be feeling.

It is common in such hard times for us to go into the "scramble mode," to rush about frantically trying to make something happen. We desperately attempt to alter our situation because we want to feel better fast. This explains why so many people in trouble make an even bigger mess of their lives by succumbing to sinful desires. They impulsively quit a good job. They foolishly enter into an illicit relationship. They hastily make an unethical decision that seems to promise immediate relief.

The Greek word translated "self-control" in today's promise refers to the holding in or restraining of our wrong passions and appetites. It is the Spirit who gives us the strength to say no to such destructive urges.

In other words, self-control is really Spirit-control.

PRAYING GOD'S PROMISE

Holy Spirit of God, I need you! I am so vulnerable, so foolish, so susceptible to sin. Keep me safe. Protect me. Open my eyes to the dangers all around me. Take my will, and make it yours, so that I do not succumb to the enticements of the world, the flesh, or the devil.

GOD'S PROMISE TO YOU

- If God's Spirit reigns in your life, he will help you to have self-control.

THE PROMISE
GOD FULFILLS YOUR HOLY PASSIONS

Take delight in the Lord, and he will give you your
heart's desires.   Psalm 37:4

HERE'S what the verse above doesn't mean: that if we immerse
ourselves in spiritual activity, God is obligated to reward us
with that new dream house we've been wanting for as long as we
can remember or bring an end to our painful struggles. Such a
way of thinking has more to do with magic than Christianity.

On the contrary, the verse serves as a reminder of the truest
things about us: we were created by and for God (Colossians
1:16); we live to bring honor to him (1 Corinthians 10:31) and
to do his perfect will (Ephesians 2:10); we have a brand-new
nature that hungers for God and that nothing in this world can
truly satisfy.

The verse echoes the truth that it's only when we let
heaven—not the stuff of earth (Colossians 3:2)—fill our
thoughts, only when we doggedly pursue the God who made us
and saved us that we find deep satisfaction of soul.

This principle is true even in the midst of tumultuous times
. . . and perhaps *especially* then.

PRAYING GOD'S PROMISE

God, I am called to delight in you. Forgive me for the times I get overly excited about things that don't matter. I want to enjoy your blessings, but I want to enjoy you and seek you more than anything else. When you become my focus and my passion, you will grant the deep desires of my heart. As your child I have a new nature. I'm not the person I used to be. Stir up the holy passions that you've put within me so that the things I want most are the things you want most to give me.

GOD'S PROMISE TO YOU

- When my desires are pure and holy, I can be sure God will grant them.

THE PROMISE
GOD GRANTS POWER TO THE WEAK

Those who wait on the Lord will find new strength. They will fly high on wings like eagles. They will run and not grow weary. They will walk and not faint.   Isaiah 40:31

AFTER a while, tough times can make you feel much like a boxer in a brutal championship bout. At first you were holding your own, even getting in a good counterpunch now and then. But for each of the last few rounds your opponent has had you trapped up against the ropes and has come close to knocking you out. Now you're slumped in your corner, so weary you don't know who or where you are. The fight's not even close to being over. People are shouting instructions and trying to give you encouragement, but if you are going to answer the bell for the next round—much less make it to the end of the fight—you'll need much more than verbal motivation.

Because that's what it feels like to go through long-term difficulty, most folks eventually lose the will to go on.

If you're worn-out and ready to throw in the towel, reflect on the promise above—that the Lord will give you renewed strength—and pray it back to God along the following lines.

PRAYING GOD'S PROMISE

Lord, your Word tells me that when I wait on you, I can find new power to persevere. Without your help I cannot live as I should. I need your limitless strength so that I can keep walking with you even in the midst of hard times. The only way to experience your strength is to wait on you. Help me learn the discipline of pausing regularly, waiting patiently, listening carefully, and drawing fully from your infinite resources.

GOD'S PROMISE TO YOU

- God gives strength to those who wait on him.
- Those who look to God and lean on him will fly high and run far; they will never run out of power.

THE PROMISE
GOD'S WORD KEEPS YOU FROM SIN

> How can a young person stay pure? By obeying your word
> and following its rules. . . . I have hidden your word in my
> heart, that I might not sin against you.   Psalm 119:9-11

IN the game of football it's called "piling on": You're already
down when suddenly you get pummeled again by your opponent. In real life it's called spiritual warfare, and it's often
disguised. You're suffering through a hard time when suddenly
the enemy comes at you with what actually looks like *relief*.

Ah, how vulnerable we are in such moments! *After all I've had
to endure lately, I think I deserve a little break!* How easy it is to
rationalize! *Would it* really *be so wrong for me to* _____? *Why
not?*

Of course, this is the nature of temptation. On the front end,
sin looks "heavenly." On the back side, it is always hellish and
makes bad situations worse.

Our only hope is in living out the promise above. By filling
our hearts and minds with the truth of God's Word, we are able
to recognize the enemy's lies. That is how we stay pure in hard,
tempting times (see Matthew 4:1-11). It is how we avoid Satan's
deceptive attempts to hit us again when we're down.

PRAYING GOD'S PROMISE

God, when I hide your Word in my heart, I can keep from sinning!
Grant me the wisdom to seek you and to hide your Word in my
heart. I need discernment to apply your truth to everyday
situations, especially when I am going through difficult times.

GOD'S PROMISE TO YOU

- God has given you his Word.
- Hiding it in your heart will keep you from wrong attitudes and
  actions.

THE PROMISE
GOD HAS SET YOU FREE IN CHRIST

Jesus said to the people who believed in him, "You are truly my disciples if you keep obeying my teachings. And you will know the truth, and the truth will set you free. . . . So if the Son sets you free, you will indeed be free."   John 8:31-32, 36

T HE federal penitentiary near Marion, Illinois, is a somber sight. Its windowless buildings, imposing guard towers, and series of barbed-wire fences remind us that the human heart is capable of great evil and that physical incarceration is a proper societal response to those who pose a threat to others.

But the promise above reminds us of a different and greater truth. Jesus offers spiritual freedom—true, ultimate liberty—to all who put their trust in him.

The freedom he brings is able to penetrate any "prison"— whether real or figurative. Hardened convicts can be released from sin's terrible penalty and power. Even weary religious folks can be unshackled from their exhausting, futile efforts to live by a million "do's and don'ts."

Don't miss this point: Christ came to set us free. Free from condemnation and shame. Free from the impossibility of trying to earn God's approval or please fickle people. Free to marvel at the wonder of forgiven sin. Free to enjoy the rich banquet of his endless grace.

So many of life's tough times can be attributed to the enslaving power of sin. Don't stay in that terrible spiritual prison, especially when Christ offers you wonderful—and complete—freedom right now.

PRAYING GOD'S PROMISE

I am truly free in Christ. What an amazing truth! But why don't I live it out? Why do I so often choose to stay locked-up in the dark prison cell of slavery to sin or slavery to the expectations of others? God, you have set me free to obey you. Teach me to believe the paradox that I am most free when I am living as your servant. Help me to better understand your grace.

GOD'S PROMISE TO YOU

- Christ's truth will set you free.
- The freedom Christ gives is true freedom.

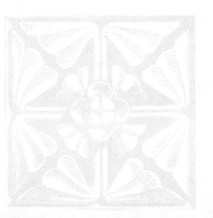

THE PROMISE
GOD MOTIVATES YOU TO KEEP DOING RIGHT

God has not given us a spirit of fear and timidity, but
of power, love, and self-discipline.   2 Timothy 1:7

EVEN people who love God and long to serve him sometimes
falter under the pressure of difficulty. Troubles can throw us for
a loop, pull the rug out from under us, and take away our will
to press on.

This was Timothy's situation. Remember him? He was Paul's
young friend and protégé, the pastor of the church at Ephesus.
From the content of the two letters that bear his name, it is
obvious that Timothy, though marked by a genuine faith,
struggled with fear, feelings of inadequacy, and complacency as
he confronted the problems in his life.

Just before departing this life, Paul wrote Timothy a final
note to remind him that God had supplied all the resources
necessary to do his will—the strength, the motivation, and the
ability to stay focused on the task.

If you're having trouble persevering, you might want to
memorize the same promise and make it your own.

PRAYING GOD'S PROMISE

I do not have to give in to the spirit of fear or timidity, Lord. I don't want to be controlled by circumstances and feelings. Forgive me for the times I live on the basis of what seems true instead of what you say is true. You provide me with power and love and self-discipline. When I turn to you, I find the necessary strength (power), the right motivation (love), and the essential will (self-discipline) I need in order to do what will bring you glory.

GOD'S PROMISE TO YOU

- God has supplied you with power.
- He has given you love.
- He has provided you with the necessary resource of self-discipline.

THE PROMISE
GOD HELPS YOU TO RESIST SIN

Remember that the temptations that come into your life are no different from what others experience. And God is faithful. He will keep the temptation from becoming so strong that you can't stand up against it. When you are tempted, he will show you a way out so that you will not give in to it.

1 Corinthians 10:13

BECAUSE of some long-term unwise spending habits, the Walkers are now facing serious financial troubles. Their economic woes have been the source of constant tension and stress at home. They have no idea how they got into this mess, much less how to get out. The thought of admitting their situation fills them with embarrassment. Interestingly, in the midst of this major money crunch:

Denise has gained some thirty pounds, is thinking about reneging on a financial commitment to her church's building campaign, and has also begun playing the lottery (something she used to call a stupid waste of money).

Donald has been escaping regularly into the world of Internet pornography while he considers partnering with an old college buddy in a "can't lose" (i.e., highly questionable) business deal.

The Walkers' situation reminds us that when we feel weakened and worried by the pressures and problems of life, certain temptations can seem irresistible.

How would *you* counsel the Walkers using the above promise of God?

PRAYING GOD'S PROMISE

My temptations are not unique. Everyone struggles. I am not alone in my struggle with sin. You, God, are faithful to protect me from "irresistible temptation." Keep me from the lame excuse that I couldn't help it. I can help it—with your help. I will never be tempted beyond what I can stand. When I am tempted, you promise to show me a way out of my dilemma. Give me sensitivity to your voice so that I do not dishonor you.

GOD'S PROMISE TO YOU

- Temptations are a fact of life.
- God is faithful to never let you be tempted more than you can endure.
- He will always provide a way for you to escape your temptations.

THE PROMISE
GOD HAS PROVIDED ALL YOU NEED

How we praise God, the Father of our Lord Jesus Christ, who
has blessed us with every spiritual blessing in the heavenly
realms because we belong to Christ.   Ephesians 1:3

MAYBE you've seen on TV the hard-core cyclists who race annu-
ally from California to New York. Averaging some twenty hours
of furious pedaling daily, these relentless athletes plow through
deserts, climb mountain ranges, cross rivers, and zip through
cities, traveling almost three thousand miles total!

How in the world do they do it? Here's the secret: Each rider
is followed by a three-to-four-person support team in a fully-
equipped RV. Everyone and everything the cyclist might need—a
coach, mechanic, massage therapist, trainer, nurse, dietitian,
chef, cheerleader, food, water, and spare bikes and parts—are
available in that chase vehicle.

In a similar but much more glorious way, God has provided
us with all the spiritual blessings we need to make it through
the most difficult parts of the race of life.

When you're exhausted and at your wit's end, it doesn't make
sense to rely only on your own limited strength and wisdom.
Why not call upon the One who has everything you need and
who will never leave your side?

PRAYING GOD'S PROMISE

God, thank you for your abundant blessings. How easy it is to forget that you are the source of every good thing and that you yourself are good. Because of Christ, I have been given every spiritual blessing I need. When I feel empty and dry, remind me that you stand ready to give me whatever I need. Teach me to value and utilize your infinite spiritual benefits and to seek after them more than after physical comforts.

GOD'S PROMISE TO YOU

- God is the God who blesses.
- He has already given you every spiritual blessing you need to live in a fallen world.

THE PROMISE
GOD GIVES YOU POWER TO LIVE RIGHT

Let heaven fill your thoughts. Do not think only about things
down here on earth. For you died when Christ died, and your
real life is hidden with Christ in God.   Colossians 3:2-3

T H E great reformers had these observations about the Christian's union with Christ:

- John Calvin: "We ought not to separate Christ from ourselves
  or ourselves from him."
- Martin Luther: "The moment I consider Christ and myself as
  two, I am gone."

This is critical truth. Through salvation God has linked us
permanently to his Son (Romans 6:1-11). Jesus is in us and with
us. We are in and with him. Being placed "in" Christ, in effect,
put to death our old nature (Galatians 2:19-20) and gave us a
new nature (2 Corinthians 5:17). The result is that we are no
longer mere creatures of earth but citizens of heaven
(Philippians 3:20). If we fail to grasp these truths, then in times
of trouble we will doubt Christ's power and presence—and likely
respond poorly.

How can pondering and claiming the promise of union with
Christ make a difference in *your* life today?

PRAYING GOD'S PROMISE

I need to change the way I think, Lord. Salvation means that somehow I was "in" Christ when he died, was buried, and was raised. Lord, these are great mysteries and profound truths. Help me to better understand the monumental blessings that result from my union with Christ. Give me thoughts of heaven so that my actions on earth are pleasing to you. Give me eyes to see and ears to hear. Give me the faith to believe this amazing promise: As a brand-new creature, I do not have to yield to sin.

GOD'S PROMISE TO YOU

- God has joined you to Christ.
- He has given you new life, *real* life, in Christ.
- Your old sinful nature is dead. It has no power over you.

THE PROMISE
GOD HELPS YOU IN PRAYER

The Holy Spirit helps us in our distress. For we don't even know what we should pray for, nor how we should pray. But the Holy Spirit prays for us with groanings that cannot be expressed in words. And the Father who knows all hearts knows what the Spirit is saying, for the Spirit pleads for us believers in harmony with God's own will.   Romans 8:26-27

IN one of the darkest moments of King Jehoshaphat's life, with a vast enemy army advancing against his nation, this ruler of the southern kingdom of Judah prayed simply, "O our God. . . . we do not know what to do, but we are looking to you for help" (2 Chronicles 20:12).

Ever feel like that? Alarmed and confused by looming troubles? Perhaps even spiritually paralyzed, so that, unlike Jehoshaphat, you feel too bewildered to compose the most basic of prayers?

If that describes you today—if you're so perplexed and upset that you don't even know how to pray—there's good news in the promise above: The Holy Spirit is praying for you! God is able to decipher the unutterable groanings of the Spirit within our spirit. And he always answers these deep, heartfelt prayers because they are always according to his will (1 John 5:14-15).

We make too much of words, worrying needlessly about composing just the "right" prayer. If we will simply lift our eyes and our souls heavenward, God will do the rest.

PRAYING GOD'S PROMISE

Lord, in my distress I don't know what to pray . . . or how. The best I can do is, "Help!" Thank you for the promise that the Holy Spirit prays for me. His pleadings are always in harmony with your will. They are for my good and your glory. Hallelujah!

GOD'S PROMISE TO YOU

- God's Spirit helps you in your distress.
- The Spirit prays for you in accordance with God's will.

THE PROMISE
GOD HAS PROVIDED AN ANTIDOTE TO WORRY

You will keep in perfect peace all who trust in you, whose thoughts are fixed on you! Trust in the Lord always, for the Lord God is the eternal Rock.   Isaiah 26:3-4

FOR many folks, concerns about bad things that *might possibly* happen are far worse than the troubles they actually end up facing. This is because the human mind is extremely creative, always busy, and unfortunately, susceptible to "the fiery arrows [of] Satan" (Ephesians 6:16).

The ancient prophet Isaiah revealed that perfect peace comes only to those who trust the Lord. Look again at his reassuring words in the verses above. This trusting process involves fixing our thoughts on God—on who he is, on what he has done, and on what he is able to do. The New Testament reiterates the importance of proactively choosing to focus our minds on God's truth (Philippians 4:8; Colossians 3:2; Hebrews 12:1-2).

The bottom line? A mind that is absorbed with the certainties of God will not have time to dwell on (and worry over) mere potentialities.

How foolish for us to create fantasy situations in our heads and then stress out over imagined scenarios! How wise for us to focus on what is . . . or, more importantly, Who is.

PRAYING GOD'S PROMISE

You promise peace to those who trust in you and set their minds on you, Lord. Maybe the reason I'm so anxious much of the time is that I lose sight of you. I focus on my problems. Forgive me. Help me to overcome this habit of faithlessness. You are solid and dependable. You are worthy of my full trust. I love you. You are my rock. So long as I look to you, I cannot be shaken.

GOD'S PROMISE TO YOU

- God will give you perfect peace when you focus on him and trust in him.
- He is the eternal Rock.

THE PROMISE
GOD GIVES CONFIRMATION
THAT YOU ARE HIS CHILD

His Holy Spirit speaks to us deep in our hearts and tells us that we are God's children.   Romans 8:16

N OTHING can send a believer into a tailspin of doubt like long-term trials or short-term crises.

Why is all this happening to me? I can't believe a loving God would let his own children go through such trauma, so maybe that means . . . I'm not really his child?

In the midst of such turmoil we need the comfort of the promise above. It is found in the midst of the apostle Paul's explanation of our spiritual adoption into God's family at salvation. For an adoption to be legal in ancient Roman culture, seven witnesses were required to attest to the validity of the proceedings.

In essence Paul is saying that the indwelling Holy Spirit is the reliable witness who confirms that we are truly God's children. How? Primarily by changing our attitudes, desires, and behavior (Galatians 5:22-23) and also by giving us new power to proclaim our faith (Acts 1:8).

If you are struggling with doubts about whether you belong to Christ, ask a friend today, "How and where do you see God at work in my life?"

PRAYING GOD'S PROMISE

Father, in times of trial I am bombarded by doubts. Tough times often make me wonder whether I really am your child. Thank you for the presence of your Spirit, who provides assurance that I belong to you. When I am struggling, give me tangible evidence that you have saved me and are changing me.

GOD'S PROMISE TO YOU

- God's Spirit provides assurance that you are his child.

THE PROMISE
GOD'S SPIRIT GIVES YOU INSIGHT

God has actually given us his Spirit (not the world's spirit) so
we can know the wonderful things God has freely given us.

1 Corinthians 2:12

QUESTION: What do people of the world do when they are
facing trouble?

Answer: Typically, they seek worldly counsel. They watch talk
shows, read advice columns, call psychics, consult horoscopes,
visit therapists, question friends, buy self-help books, and/or
attend assorted seminars.

A Danish proverb illustrates the problem with such a
haphazard approach: "He who builds to every man's advice will
have a crooked house."

That is not to say that *all* of the above sources of counsel are
always wrong. No, the point here is that there is a much more
reliable and excellent source of wisdom. He's called the Holy
Spirit, and he lives inside everyone who believes in Jesus Christ.

The question then is, Why would any Christian settle for
fallible counsel and insight when he or she already has internal
access to infallible truth and knowledge?

If you've got questions, the Spirit has answers. And remember, one piece of good advice is better than a whole bagful of
foolish counsel.

PRAYING GOD'S PROMISE

You have given me your Holy Spirit. Thank you, Lord! What would I do without your presence in my life? Forgive my foolish habit of not stopping to hear what you are saying, of not letting you teach me and guide me. Only your Spirit can help me understand all the spiritual blessings you have given me. Teach me how to listen to you. Give me ears to hear. I need to better understand you and all your good gifts to me. Draw me closer to you.

GOD'S PROMISE TO YOU

- God has given you his Spirit.
- God's Spirit will show you the depths of his blessings.

THE PROMISE
GOD QUENCHES YOUR THIRSTY SOUL

> Jesus said, "The water I give . . . takes away thirst alto-
> gether. It becomes a perpetual spring within them, giving . . .
> eternal life."
>
> John 4:14

THE renowned British author C. S. Lewis once observed that if we find within ourselves longings that nothing in this world can satisfy, the only logical conclusion is that we were created for another world.

Of course, we *do* have those longings—all of us. Look around you. Look at all the fidgety, searching people. Look at the countless ways people try to fill the gnawing emptiness inside them. Look into your own heart, which never quite feels at home in this world.

Now, observe Jesus of Nazareth, standing at Jacob's well conversing with a woman with a dried-up spirit. Listen as he proclaims himself the solution for her soul's deepest longings.

Tough times provide the unexpected blessing of putting restless people in touch with their soul's desperate condition. If you can relate to such spiritual thirst, accept Jesus' offer of living water. Your problems likely will not change, but you will.

PRAYING GOD'S PROMISE

Jesus, you are the only One who can satisfy those who thirst. I need to remember that nothing in a temporal world can bring lasting fulfillment to my immortal soul. The life that you give supplies continual refreshment. Teach me the holy habit of looking to you alone for whatever my spirit is thirsty for. Make me a source of encouragement and help to those who are spiritually dry.

GOD'S PROMISE TO YOU

- God alone can quench your spiritual thirst.
- He gives eternal life.

PART 4

LOOKING AHEAD:
THE FUTURE WE SEE

CENTURIES ago, a mystic known as John of the Cross said, "See that you are not suddenly saddened by the adversities of this world, for you do not know the good they bring, being ordained in the judgments of God for the everlasting joy of the elect."

These profound words remind us that in ways we cannot fully understand, God *is* at work in and through our troubles. A glorious future awaits those who respond to life's difficulties with God-honoring faithfulness. These final thirty devotions give us a game plan for tough times. They encourage us to persevere, to live out our Christian responsibilities with the confidence that it pays—eternally!—to cling in simple faith to the trustworthy promises of God.

THE PROMISE
GOD IS MAKING YOU LIKE JESUS

As the Spirit of the Lord works within us, we become more
and more like him and reflect his glory even more.

2 Corinthians 3:18

I T begins as a big, shapeless block of marble. Over an extended period of time the sculptor chips and chisels, shapes and smoothes. At last the day comes for the great unveiling. The giant covering is yanked away, and there stands a breathtaking, lifelike masterpiece—a reflection of the artist's genius and character.

In effect, this is what God is doing in and with us. He is the great craftsman, dedicated to taking our ordinary, unimpressive lives and transforming them into unique and eternal works of art. More precisely, he is about the business of making us just like his Son (Romans 8:29; 1 John 3:2).

The process itself is painstaking and painful. But the point (the glory of God) and the product (a fully redeemed and re-created life) make it worth whatever price we must pay.

Writer Philip Yancey asks: "Who would complain if God allowed one hour of suffering in an entire lifetime of comfort? Why complain about a lifetime that includes suffering when that lifetime is a mere hour of eternity?"

PRAYING GOD'S PROMISE

Father, thank you for loving me enough to work in me. Make me aware of your presence. Make me cooperative with your indwelling Spirit. Keep me from complaining. Your goal is to change me so that I reflect your glory. I can't always see signs of change, but I pray that others can. Mostly I pray that you can. May you increase, and may I decrease.

GOD'S PROMISE TO YOU

- God's Spirit is working in you.
- He is making you like Christ so that you will reflect his glory.

THE PROMISE
GOD'S CHILDREN WILL FACE TROUBLE
IN THIS LIFE

It is actually best for you that I go away, because if I don't,
the Counselor won't come. If I do go away, he will come
because I will send him to you.   John 16:7

A lot of Christians are disappointed or even disillusioned in
their faith because somewhere along the line they bought into
the popular fallacy that being a child of God guarantees a life of
unending blessing: health, wealth, comfort, ease, etc.

Nothing could be further from the truth. The Old Testament
saint Job correctly observed, "People are born for trouble as
predictably as sparks fly upward from a fire" (Job 5:7). Indeed,
suffering is a fact of life in a fallen world.

Consider the names and descriptions of the Holy Spirit. Jesus
described him as our Counselor. Other passages and/or Bible
translations call him our Helper, our Comforter, and the One
who intercedes for us. Such terms and phrases clearly imply
that we will routinely find ourselves in desperate situations.

We need to adjust our expectations accordingly. We *will* face
trouble—but we will never be alone. Are you calling upon and
depending on the Spirit in your tough times, or are you ignor-
ing his presence in your life?

PRAYING GOD'S PROMISE

I should never be surprised by trouble, Lord. Both the Bible and human experience indicate that we should expect hard times in this life. Thank you for sending your Spirit. I do not go through difficulty alone. You are with me always—to counsel, to help, and to pray for me.

GOD'S PROMISE TO YOU

- God's Spirit will be with you in all your times of trouble.

THE PROMISE
GOD WILL GIVE YOU PERFECT COUNSEL

If you need wisdom—if you want to know what God wants you to do—ask him, and he will gladly tell you. He will not resent your asking.

James 1:5

F o r at least two generations now, millions of desperate and confused people have sought guidance from the syndicated columnists Ann Landers and Abigail "Abby" Van Buren, who happen to be twin sisters. Every now and then these famous counselors manage to offer decent advice. But often their suggestions are unsound and outrageous. Are Ann and Abby the best we can do?

No, not by a long shot.

If we want surefire counsel based in truth, if we want guidance that works, we need the wisdom that comes straight from God. That's what the apostle James tells us in the passage above, and interestingly, he cites this promise in the middle of a discussion about how to handle hard times.

If you're scratching your head as you ponder your next move, take your questions to God himself. As you listen to the Word and to the Spirit, you'll eventually know the best course of action.

PRAYING GOD'S PROMISE

Lord, when times get tough, it is hard to know what to do. I need wisdom from above. I praise you for being the source of all wisdom. I thank you for being patient. You are glad to help me. You do not resent my requests. Help me to remember your willingness to help in my times of trial. You promise to tell me what I need to do. What wonderful assurance! I do not have to navigate my way through my troubles alone.

GOD'S PROMISE TO YOU

- God will give you wisdom.
- He will gladly show you what to do.
- He will never be irritated by your request for insight.

THE PROMISE
GOD HAS A PLAN FOR YOU

I cry out to God Most High, to God who will fulfill his purpose
for me.   Psalm 57:2

T HE most famous and most distributed gospel tract in the
world, Campus Crusade's *The Four Spiritual Laws,* begins with
these words: "God loves you and has a wonderful plan for your
life."

What a great reminder of the truth that God has a unique
purpose for each of us. Yes, he has plans for you—a special place
for you to fit, a key role for you to play in his divine drama.

This is true no matter what trials you're facing right now. In
fact, because of God's sovereignty (see devotion 47) we know
that even our messes are somehow a part of God's cosmic
plotline!

David grasped this truth, as we see in today's promise. As a
result, he was able to look heavenward and express his trust in
God in a time of great personal trouble.

God will fulfill his purpose for you! He really does have a
wonderful plan for your life.

Latch on to this extraordinary promise today.

PRAYING GOD'S PROMISE

God, in the midst of tough times, it's tough to remember that you're in control. But you are the most high God. You sit enthroned above the heavens. You rule over all things. I praise you because you will fulfill your purpose in my life. Instead of complaining and doubting, I want to wait patiently for your goodness and trust confidently in your infinite power.

GOD'S PROMISE TO YOU

● God will fulfill his purpose in your life.

THE PROMISE
GOD WILL HONOR YOUR INTEGRITY

Day by day the Lord takes care of the innocent, and they will
receive a reward that lasts forever.   Psalm 37:18

MAYBE last month it was a relational disaster or an occupa-
tional trial. This week it might be a financial setback. Next week
could bring a health crisis. After a while the unrelenting stream
of tough times takes its toll.

"What's the use?" we cry. "I try to do right and for what? Life
keeps beating me up! I can't get ahead! I'm not sure it pays to
try to live a godly life. I struggle as much or more than my
neighbors who couldn't care less about God!"

Troubles certainly have a way of wearing us down. And if
we're not careful, they can erode even our bedrock convictions.
The promise above is a good reminder of why we must be vigi-
lant about not taking moral or ethical shortcuts.

Those who maintain their integrity, those who continue to
do right even when everything and everyone else is wrong will
one day receive the ultimate reward.

PRAYING GOD'S PROMISE

Life doesn't seem fair at times, Lord, and integrity often doesn't seem to matter. But it does matter. You see everything. Nothing escapes your gaze. You promise to care for the pure and to reward the faithful. Give me the spiritual tenacity to hang in there. Remind me that the day is coming when you will exalt those who steadfastly trust in you.

GOD'S PROMISE TO YOU

- God will take care of his innocent children.
- You will receive an eternal reward.

THE PROMISE
GOD HAS DETERMINED THE LENGTH
OF YOUR LIFE

Lord, remind me how brief my time on earth will be. Remind me that my days are numbered, and that my life is fleeing away. My life is no longer than the width of my hand. An entire lifetime is just a moment to you; human existence is but a breath. Psalm 39:4-5

A T some deep level we do realize we're mortal creatures. However, most of us on most days avoid such thoughts. We might mention getting older or comment on how time flies, but then we quickly change the subject. We whistle past graveyards because the brevity of life is, frankly, a sobering and unnerving topic.

And yet the promise that God has allotted each of us a specific number of days—no more and no less—is a life-changing, even freeing truth. It gives us much-needed perspective, especially in the midst of hard times.

"This too"—this struggle, this difficulty, this stress—"shall pass." Let each flip of the calendar remind you that this pain-filled existence is not all there is. Greater things await. God is eternal, but tough times are not.

An old saying by an unknown saint is worth meditating on today: "Only one life, 'twill soon be past. Only what's done for Christ will last."

PRAYING GOD'S PROMISE

Remind me, God, that my days are numbered. This promise motivates me, Lord, to live wisely and well. I want to make each day count, for I have only a set number. Grip me with the reality of your eternality—and the brevity of my earthly life.

GOD'S PROMISE TO YOU

- God has given you a set number of days.

THE PROMISE
GOD TURNS TROUBLE INTO TRIUMPH

Our present troubles are quite small and won't last very long. Yet they produce for us an immeasurably great glory that will last forever! So we don't look at the troubles we can see right now; rather, we look forward to what we have not yet seen. For the troubles we see will soon be over, but the joys to come will last forever.   2 Corinthians 4:17-18

A few fortunate women have "effortless" pregnancies—no morning sickness, plenty of energy, minimal weight gain—that culminate in quick deliveries and recoveries. The average woman, however, struggles with some combination of nausea, weariness, back pain, wild mood swings, a long, torturous labor, and perhaps even a medical complication or two along the way. For this majority of women nine months can seem like nine years.

Yet the old clichés are true. The teary-eyed mom holding her newborn is quick to admit, "It's worth every bit of the trouble." All the discomfort and stress are swallowed up by the joy of new life.

This is the idea in the apostle Paul's words about our temporal struggles. From our vantage point, tough times seem gigantic, endless, and pointless. But by the light of eternity we will one day see them as "quite small," short-lived, and responsible for immeasurable good.

It is this kind of thinking—looking ahead, anticipating the lasting joy that God will bring forth from your temporal troubles—that will get you through your tough times.

PRAYING GOD'S PROMISE

It takes great faith to read today's passage with real conviction. My troubles seem huge, Lord. Give me eyes to see how temporary my trials are and how eternal your blessings are. Give me the discipline to focus on the bright future you have promised me.

GOD'S PROMISE TO YOU

- In the light of eternity your troubles are insignificant and temporary.
- God will give you a joy that lasts forever.

THE PROMISE
GOD PROVIDES HAPPINESS AS YOU LIVE
BY HIS WORD

Make me walk along the path of your commands, for that is
where my happiness is found.   Psalm 119:35

THE Bible frequently pictures our earthly existence as a foot
journey. In other words, we "walk" through this life. And as we
do, we must choose. We can join the throng of travelers on the
popular, broad roads that ignore the Creator and lead ultimately to destruction, or we can choose, with the dwindling
minority, to walk with the Lord (Matthew 7:13-14).

Choosing Christ means a tough, often lonely trip along a
narrow path. This way—i.e., his way—will take us straight into
dangerous territory. We will have frightening moments.
Appealing yet misleading shortcuts will tempt us repeatedly. We
will, on occasion, feel lost—or feel that all is lost.

But in truth, we are safest and happiest when we stay on
Christ's path, walking along the way outlined in the Word of
God. This plodding life seldom brings the thrills that we might
find at an amusement park. But it results in a lasting happiness
that most travelers will never know.

PRAYING GOD'S PROMISE

This world offers an endless variety of life paths. Lord, help me to see that true happiness is found in walking with you. I want the narrow way of Christ, not the broad path that leads to destruction. Give me a hunger for your Word and a passion to live it out in my daily existence.

GOD'S PROMISE TO YOU

- You will find happiness to the degree that you obey God's Word.

THE PROMISE
GOD COMFORTS US SO WE CAN
COMFORT OTHERS

[God] comforts us in all our troubles so that we can comfort others. When others are troubled, we will be able to give them the same comfort God has given us. You can be sure that the more we suffer for Christ, the more God will shower us with his comfort through Christ.   2 Corinthians 1:4-5

IF we're honest, what we'd really like is deliverance *from* our troubles. We want all our problems to go away and never come back. One day we'll get that wish—in a place called heaven. But for now, the best we can hope for is comfort *in the midst of* our pain.

The verb "comforts" that Paul used to describe God's response in our times of calamity conveys the idea of being called alongside. In other words, when we're at our lowest point, God shows up, often in a quiet, almost imperceptible way. He provides consolation and encouragement and strength through a hug from a Christian friend, a song lyric, a Bible verse that jumps off the page, an encouraging letter or e-mail. All of these are the work of God, his tools of consolation to enable you to keep going.

And what do you do with that renewed strength? God wants *you* to come alongside someone else in pain and pass along the encouragement you've received.

PRAYING GOD'S PROMISE

You comfort me in all my troubles. Thank you for caring for me, Lord. Make me more aware of your consoling work in my life. You want me to come alongside others who hurt. Deliver me from the tendency to be self-absorbed. I want to be a conduit of your encouragement and a strengthener of my brothers and sisters. Help me to be your hands and feet to others who are hurting.

GOD'S PROMISE TO YOU

- God will comfort you in all your troubles.
- He will use you to come alongside others who are hurting.

THE PROMISE
GOD USES HARD TIMES TO GET OUR ATTENTION

The suffering you sent was good for me, for it taught me to pay attention to your principles.   Psalm 119:71

IF difficulties merely strengthen a prideful reliance on our own human strength and will . . .

- if personal pain becomes our obsession, and relieving it becomes our chief goal in life . . .
- if our troubles serve only to drive us to bitterness and envy and despair . . .

then we have squandered a wonderful opportunity to know God better.

In *The Problem of Pain,* the brilliant British author C. S. Lewis once wrote: "God whispers to us in our pleasures, speaks to us in our conscience, but shouts in our pains: it is His megaphone to rouse a deaf world."[1] In another place, Lewis called suffering God's "severe mercy."

If you are hurting, stop looking around. Cease looking for answers within yourself. Resist the temptation to become angry and sullen. Instead, look up. God is trying to get your attention. He wants to reveal himself and his truth to you.

This is how suffering becomes a blessing in our lives.

PRAYING GOD'S PROMISE

*You use suffering in my life to get my attention, Lord. Forgive me
for missing the point, for complaining and pouting, for accusing you
of being cruel and indifferent. You are wise and good. Suffering is
never enjoyable, but it can be profitable in my life if I don't fight it.
Help me to learn the lessons you have for me.*

GOD'S PROMISE TO YOU

● God uses suffering to get you focused on what's true.

[1] C. S. Lewis, *The Problem of Pain* (New York: Macmillan, 1962), 93.

THE PROMISE
GOD WORKS BEST IN OUR TROUBLES

Each time he said, "My gracious favor is all you need. My power works best in your weakness." So now I am glad to boast about my weaknesses, so that the power of Christ may work through me.   2 Corinthians 12:9

THE apostle Paul had a significant problem, something he labeled a "thorn in my flesh." Was it a physical ailment? an emotional condition? external persecution? No one really knows, although Bible scholars have lots of theories. All we can say for sure is that this "thorn" was the source of much anguish.

Paul begged God repeatedly for relief from his desperate situation. God repeatedly said no. And so Paul found himself in an uncomfortable corner where he had no choice but to rely humbly on God. When he quit fighting, this weak, wounded man became a powerful servant for the Lord.

The same strength—God's strength—is available to you right now. But you experience such life-changing grace only when you accept your situation as from God and depend fully on God's infinite resources.

In proclaiming this truth, minister and U.S. Senate chaplain Peter Marshall prayed this way: "When we long for life without difficulties, remind us that oaks grow strong in contrary winds and diamonds are made under pressure."

PRAYING GOD'S PROMISE

God, your power is displayed most clearly in my inability. Be glorified in me as I humbly lean on you and wait for you to work. Help me to remember that when I can't, you can. This is the paradox of the faith—the magnificent power of God at work in the life of a helpless creature like me!

GOD'S PROMISE TO YOU

- God's grace is all you need.
- His power works best in your weakness.
- Tough times are prime opportunities for you to trust God and see him work.

THE PROMISE
GOD USES PURE SERVANTS

If you keep yourself pure, you will be a utensil God can use for his purpose. Your life will be clean, and you will be ready for the Master to use you for every good work.   2 Timothy 2:21

"Don't just sit there twiddling your thumbs, make yourself useful!"

It's the sort of blunt remark you might hear a grandparent say. A plainspoken rebuke of passivity and self-absorption. A sharp reminder of work to be done.

In so many words, this is the message of the New Testament letter we call 2 Timothy. Like us, Timothy wrestled with a host of pressures and trials. Like us, Timothy was tempted in the face of difficulty to retreat into self-pity and inactivity. Just before Paul's execution, he fired off one last letter to his young, timid colleague and friend: Don't just sit there, Timothy! There's kingdom work to be done! Make yourself useful! How? you ask. By staying clean, by saying no to sin, and by saying yes to God.

Almost two thousand years later it's still very wise advice.

Are you living a pure life so that the Master can use you? Are you staying busy for him?

PRAYING GOD'S PROMISE

You want to use me for your purposes, God, to do big things. Thank you for allowing me to participate in your eternal plan. Only if I am clean will you choose to work through me. Show me any failures or wrong choices that I need to see, admit, and turn from. I want to be clean. I want you to use me. Make me usable.

GOD'S PROMISE TO YOU

- God desires to use you.
- If you are spiritually pure, he will use you to accomplish his will.

THE PROMISE
GOD IS MAKING YOU HOLY

Now you are free from the power of sin and have become
slaves of God. Now you do those things that lead to holiness
and result in eternal life.   Romans 6:22

Sanctified is a religious word Christians don't use much
anymore. It means, literally, "to be set apart" for God's special
use. It reminds us that only that which has been made holy can
serve a holy God.

Holiness happens, in one sense, when we trust in Jesus
Christ, recognizing his death on the cross as the only sufficient
payment for our sins. At that moment we become "set apart" in
the eyes of God. We are no longer regarded as common and
corrupt. We are actually *sanctified*—made pure and holy in the
fullest, most eternal sense of those words.

Then comes the messy business of *practical* holiness; that is,
learning to live out our new, true nature. Pure attitudes,
God-honoring decisions, holy habits—these marks of a sanctified life take a lifetime to develop.

Whether we like it or not, trials are some of the most effective
tools God has in his relentless quest to set us apart. If trouble is
what it takes to transform us, trouble is what God will allow us
to experience.

PRAYING GOD'S PROMISE

I have been freed from the power of sin. I praise you, God, for making me holy. Because of Christ I am clean and acceptable in your sight. I am called to live my life as your "sanctified" slave. As I encounter difficulties today, I want to respond in ways that "set me apart" from my old ways of thinking and living. Let me live to your glory.

GOD'S PROMISE TO YOU

- God has freed you from the power of sin.
- You are his slave.
- He is making you holy.

THE PROMISE
GOD GRANTS YOU OVERCOMING POWER

We can rejoice, too, when we run into problems and trials, for we know that they are good for us they help us learn to endure. And endurance develops strength of character in us, and character strengthens our confident expectation of salvation.

Romans 5:3-4

IN his memoir *Telling Secrets,* writer Frederick Buechner writes vividly of his daughter's near-death struggle with anorexia, concluding, "The fearsome blessing of that hard time continues to work itself out in my life."[2]

"Fearsome"? Yes, of course! "Hard time"? Without a doubt! But "blessing"? Such a word in such a context seems oxymoronic, even moronic—unless we believe promises such as the one above.

In heaven's strange economy, bad can be converted to good (Romans 8:28). Trials in our lives are subject to a kind of cosmic reversal. They will not kill us; on the contrary, if we endure, they serve to make us stronger and better.

The verb Paul uses for "endure" means literally "to remain under." Maybe a good picture is the football player who is straining under a five-hundred-pound barbell. For now the weight is "fearsome," nothing but sheer agony and struggle. But in time the experience will result in "blessing," providing new strength to overcome new obstacles.

PRAYING GOD'S PROMISE

My problems and trials sure don't seem good, Lord. And yet you tell me you are using them for my good. I want to learn to endure so that I demonstrate the character of a true child of God. Give me the gritty determination to "remain under" my trials until they accomplish your will. Keep me from grumbling. Make me a joyful sufferer.

GOD'S PROMISE TO YOU

- God is using your struggles to teach you to endure.
- He is committed to making you Christlike in your character.

[2]Frederick Buechner, *Telling Secrets* (San Francisco: HarperCollins, 1991), 24.

THE PROMISE
GOD GIVES VICTORY OVER WORRY

Don't worry about anything; instead, pray about everything. Tell God what you need, and thank him for all he has done. If you do this, you will experience God's peace, which is far more wonderful than the human mind can understand. His peace will guard your hearts and minds as you live in Christ Jesus.

Philippians 4:6-7

IT'S no wonder people cross-stitch, frame, and memorize this passage so frequently—the promise is for peace, true peace, *God's* peace. The assurance is for a supernatural calmness of soul that defies our comprehension and boggles our imagination. The guarantee is an inner tranquillity that steels our shaky hearts and minds against all the what-ifs the world can throw at us.

So how do we get this peace? What's *our* role in experiencing such supernatural serenity?

We replace fretful thoughts with prayer. We look to God. All the time. In every situation. And as we do, as we thankfully remember all the past times when God has faithfully worked and provided and helped, we sense our souls relaxing.

In the words of French novelist Victor Hugo, "Have courage for the great sorrows of life and patience for the small ones; and when you have laboriously accomplished your daily task, go to sleep in peace. God is awake."

PRAYING GOD'S PROMISE

You call me to wonder and worship, not to worry, Lord. I'm sorry for not trusting you. Forgive me for foolishly acting as though I am the CEO of the universe. I can't control anything—except my decisions. Guard my heart and mind with your wonderful peace. Oh God, give me the wisdom and discipline to rein in my mind. Teach me the art of praying without ceasing.

GOD'S PROMISE TO YOU

- God will give you peace.
- His peace will guard your heart and mind as you trust him.

THE PROMISE
GOD GRANTS YOU THE ABILITY TO
HANG IN THERE

I can do everything with the help of Christ who gives me the
strength I need.   Philippians 4:13

L IKE most folks, the apostle Paul had his share of financial ups
and downs. He speaks openly of his experience in the last few
paragraphs of his letter to the church at Philippi. His comments
are wise and helpful for anyone facing hard times, fiscal or
otherwise.

He acknowledges having "plenty" on certain occasions and
"almost nothing" in the way of financial resources at other
times (Philippians 4:12). But notice that even in his bleakest
moments, when his stomach was literally empty and growling,
Paul's spirit was full (v. 11). Paul experienced genuine content-
ment in difficult times. How did he do this?

Paul relied on the strength of Christ to get him through. The
verb translated "gives me . . . strength" means to infuse needed
power into our souls. God's strength is a persevering kind of
divine energy that can sustain you through economic difficulties or troubles of any kind.

In what part of your life do you need a boost of divine help
and strength today?

PRAYING GOD'S PROMISE

I need help, Lord, and you have promised to infuse me with your infinite power. Without divine assistance I cannot press on. With your help and strength, I can do whatever you ask of me. Give me a second wind. I look to you in trust because I know you are faithful.

GOD'S PROMISE TO YOU

- God will help you.
- He will give you the strength you need.
- You will be able to do whatever is necessary.

THE PROMISE
GOD SUPPLIES EVERYTHING YOU NEED

This same God who takes care of me will supply all your
needs from his glorious riches, which have been given to us in
Christ Jesus.   Philippians 4:19

T HE first century Christians at Philippi were a generous group.
On several occasions they collected and sent financial aid to the
apostle Paul. Later, when they learned that Paul was in a Roman
prison, they promptly dispatched Epaphroditus to express their
concern and to present a large financial gift to make Paul's
incarceration more bearable (v. 18).

Perhaps all this giving severely depleted their own material
resources. Or maybe the economy in Macedonia took a turn for
the worse. Whatever the case, the implication of the last few
paragraphs in Philippians is that these openhanded believers
suddenly were facing financial needs of their own.

Paul's inspired words contain a wonderful promise: God *will*
provide for his children. The verse also reminds us of the divine
law of reciprocity stated elsewhere: "Honor the Lord with your
wealth and with the best part of everything your land produces.
Then he will fill your barns with grain, and your vats will overflow with the finest wine" (Proverbs 3:9-10).

PRAYING GOD'S PROMISE

Lord, you pledge to meet the needs of your children. Keep me from being stingy—with my time, my treasure, or my talents. Deepen my conviction that I can give myself and my "stuff" freely and fully and that you will be faithful to provide all I need out of your glorious riches.

GOD'S PROMISE TO YOU

- God will supply all your needs.

THE PROMISE
GOD USES SORROW FOR HIS PURPOSES

God can use sorrow in our lives to help us turn away from sin and seek salvation. We will never regret that kind of sorrow. But sorrow without repentance is the kind that results in death.

2 Corinthians 7:10

WHEN most people think of tough times, they think of physical or financial trouble. But what about spiritual difficulty; specifically, what about those occasions in life when we become aware of the wrongness of certain attitudes or actions?

Second Corinthians 7 addresses this topic of spiritual sorrow. The apostle Paul had previously written a stern letter to the church at Corinth, rebuking them for certain wrong actions. They might have become hostile in the face of such confrontation, or they might have reacted with worldly regret (i.e., the self-centered, superficial remorse at having been caught).

Instead, they reacted with true godly sorrow. They saw their sin in all its ugliness, saw it as an affront to a holy God. From this place of genuine spiritual sorrow, they humbly sought forgiveness and the power to change.

God can use sorrow for our good and for his glory but not if we are hard-hearted and hardheaded.

PRAYING GOD'S PROMISE

Thank you, Lord, for the deep conviction of soul that you bring into my life. A guilty conscience proves that you love me, and it points me back to you. I want to respond to your convicting work with humility and repentance. Keep me from the snare of being sad about sin's unpleasant consequences but not sorrowful over the sin itself.

GOD'S PROMISE TO YOU

- God uses spiritual regret in your life to bring you back to him.

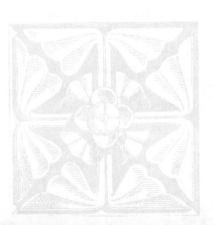

THE PROMISE
GOD'S DEVOTION TO YOU IS UNCONDITIONAL

If we are unfaithful, he remains faithful, for he cannot deny
himself.   2 Timothy 2:13

W HAT'S your favorite hymn or praise song? Why? Is it the
music? the beat? the lyrics? all of the above?

In 2 Timothy 2, the apostle Paul quoted some lines from
what most scholars believe was an early Christian hymn.
Perhaps Paul and Timothy had sung it together on various
ministry trips. Maybe Paul remembered its special meaning to
Timothy. Whatever the case, the soon-to-be-executed mission-
ary used these lyrics to challenge his young friend to keep walking with God even in life's hardest moments.

The last line, the one quoted above, is important. It's a
reminder that even when our commitment wavers, God remains
fully committed to us. Our faithlessness does not in any way
alter his faithfulness.

God is not going anywhere; he is with us to the end. What a
comforting promise for fickle followers! And what a motivation
to sing our favorite hymns of praise! God is worthy of your
worship—especially in the tough times of life.

PRAYING GOD'S PROMISE

Even when I am unfaithful, Lord, you are not. I praise you for being my faithful God. Nothing can cause you to give up on me. You always keep your promises. Father, let me live to your glory today in the realization of your perfect love and care.

GOD'S PROMISE TO YOU

- God will not turn his back on you, no matter what.

THE PROMISE
GOD'S LOVE FOR YOU CONTINUES FOREVER

Can anything ever separate us from Christ's love? Does it mean
he no longer loves us if we have trouble or calamity, or are
persecuted, or are hungry or cold or in danger or threatened
with death? . . . No.   Romans 8:35-37

O NE of the fascinating subplots in the Oscar-winning movie
Rocky is the way in which the shy and homely Adrian, played by
Talia Shire, blossoms in response to the title character's
awkward affection. The result is a vivid picture of the transforming power of unconditional love.

This is not just Hollywood fantasy. To an infinite degree this
is the promise of the gospel. Believers are chosen (i.e., hand-
picked) by God. In Christ, we are fully accepted. As God's children, we are absolutely cherished. The Father is eternally
committed to us—with no conditions. And the inspired words
of Paul, above, assure us that nothing in the universe can alter
this stunning fact.

God's love, properly understood, gives us supreme confidence. It not only provides a safety net, but it also gives us
wings. We have absolutely nothing to fear.

Regardless of how things seem right now, you are on God's
heart and mind. You are the target of his perfect love.

PRAYING GOD'S PROMISE

Nothing can ever separate me from your love. God, this seems too good to be true! Enable me to grasp the reality of your impossible-to-comprehend love. In my darkest moments keep me going with this truth. And ultimately, I ask you to use it to transform me.

GOD'S PROMISE TO YOU

- Nothing in all the universe can keep God from loving you.

THE PROMISE
GOD TAKES CARE OF TOMORROW

Your heavenly Father already knows all your needs, and he
will give you all you need from day to day if you live for him
and make the Kingdom of God your primary concern. So don't
worry about tomorrow, for tomorrow will bring its own worries.

Matthew 6:32-34

HERE'S an interesting exercise: On a blank sheet of paper, draw
three circles: one to represent how you view your past, one to
illustrate your life right now, and one to symbolize how you see
your future.

If you're like a lot of people, your "past" and "future" circles
will be larger than your "present" circle. Why? Because we tend
to agonize over our past and/or obsess about our future.
Between regret, guilt, and shame over what has been and fear
and worry about what might be, we don't have time or energy
left to enjoy what is.

Christ calls us to a new mind-set: forgetting the past
(Philippians 3:13) and entrusting tomorrow to the One who
holds the future. When God gave his people manna in the
desert (Exodus 16), they were not to try to stockpile this heavenly bread. They were not to worry about the next day's food,
only enjoy today's supply.

Jesus wants you to live in the "now." And why not? Today is all you have. Trust your faithful Father with your uncertain tomorrow.

PRAYING GOD'S PROMISE

Lord, you know all my needs and promise to meet them. I am comforted by the truth that you know every detail of my current situation. Nothing catches you off guard—ever. Thank you for being so good. I experience your promise of daily provision as I make your kingdom my top concern. Help me to seek you first, to trust your promise, to live in the "now," and to stop worrying about tomorrow.

GOD'S PROMISE TO YOU

- God knows your needs.
- He will meet all your daily needs as you live for him.

THE PROMISE
GOD GUARANTEES YOU A WONDERFUL FUTURE

> I pray that your hearts will be flooded with light so that you can understand the wonderful future he has promised to those he called.
>
> Ephesians 1:18

F OR just a few minutes, play "meteorologist," and based on *your* reading of the signs, give a weather forecast for your life.

As best you can tell, what's ahead? Hazy conditions? Heat advisories? Cloudy skies? Severe thunderstorms? Hail? (Southern readers need to be especially careful how they say this!) Tornado warnings? A winter storm watch?

Whatever uncertainties you're facing, regardless of the ominous conditions looming on the horizon of your life or even the storms raging all about you right now, the promise above offers real hope. Things might get worse before they get better, but they will get better. The Lord guarantees his children a "wonderful future."

Ask God for the insight to see the truth of this promise and the faith to cling to it when the "weather" of your life turns really nasty. Ask especially for faith. In the words of inventor C. F. Kettering, "No one ever would have crossed the ocean if he could have gotten off the ship in the storm."

PRAYING GOD'S PROMISE

I do need light, Lord. Help me to see not just my present troubles but the future you have planned for me. Flood my heart with your light. You assure me that a wonderful future awaits. Help me to have a long-term perspective. Keep me from impatience and faithlessness. When troubles come, remind me that I'm not home yet and that the day is coming when you will wipe away every tear and bring an end to all mourning and pain.

GOD'S PROMISE TO YOU

- God has a wonderful future planned for you.

THE PROMISE
GOD SUSTAINS THOSE WITH DEVOTED HEARTS

The eyes of the Lord search the whole earth in order to
strengthen those whose hearts are fully committed to him.

2 Chronicles 16:9

KING Asa of Judah was in a jam. With the armies of Israel bearing down on him from the north, Asa formed a hasty alliance with the godless Syrians. From a purely human standpoint, it might have been his best move. From heaven's vantage point, it was an act of faithlessness.

Enter Hanani the prophet. He reminded Asa of the truth above and sternly added, "What a fool you have been! From now on, you will be at war."

This avoidable episode is a sober warning to all who face trouble. God is watching. He is looking for those who are "fully committed to him." This Hebrew phrase suggests a mind that is made up, an inner resolve to trust, a steely will that is determined to do only what is pleasing to God. When the Lord finds this kind of fierce devotion, he strengthens and helps.

Don't be a fickle believer who is committed to Christ only when life is easy and good. Catch God's eye (and discover his infinite strength) by being a faithful follower of the Lord through thick and thin.

PRAYING GOD'S PROMISE

You are watching, looking, searching, Lord. You see all things. You see my heart. I pray that you are pleased by what you see. You strengthen those with a radical commitment to you. May my problems drive me into your arms, where I can find real help. Keep me from the curse of a halfhearted faith. Give me a burning passion to please you.

GOD'S PROMISE TO YOU

- God sees all the affairs of earth.
- He strengthens those whose hearts are fully devoted to him.

THE PROMISE
GOD HAS MADE YOU HIS AMBASSADOR

> God was in Christ, reconciling the world to himself, no longer counting people's sins against them. This is the wonderful message he has given us to tell others. We are Christ's ambassadors.
>
> 2 Corinthians 5:19-20

T HIS passage highlights one of the major themes of the New Testament: the idea that *all* Christians have a responsibility to both practice and proclaim their faith. Evangelism is not optional.

But what about when hard times come? Don't we get a break? Aren't we exempt from the great commission, at least until our lives calm down?

Not really. Trials aren't an excuse for not sharing our faith; on the contrary, they are an opportunity to speak out for God. The apostle Paul says as much in the next chapter of 2 Corinthians: "We patiently endure troubles and hardships and calamities of every kind. We have been beaten, been put in jail, faced angry mobs, worked to exhaustion, endured sleepless nights, and gone without food. We have proved ourselves by our purity, our understanding, our patience, our kindness, our sincere love, and the power of the Holy Spirit. *We have faithfully preached the truth. God's power has been working in us*" (2 Corinthians 6:4-7, emphasis added).

Trials didn't stop Paul from announcing the Good News. They should not deter us either.

PRAYING GOD'S PROMISE

God, you have given the gospel to me so that I might show it and share it. Thank you for forgiving my sin. Forgive me for the times I've been tight-lipped about my faith. I am your ambassador. Help me to see beyond my problems today to my real purpose: living for you and representing you. Give me creativity in using my struggles to speak for you.

GOD'S PROMISE TO YOU

- God has forgiven your sin and reconciled you to himself.
- He has given you the Good News to share with others.
- You are his ambassador.

THE PROMISE
GOD HONORS YOUR FAITH

So, you see, it is impossible to please God without faith. Anyone who wants to come to him must believe that there is a God and that he rewards those who sincerely seek him.

Hebrews 11:6

W ITH coaches and teammates shouting instructions, the five-year-old in the oversized batting helmet swings with all his might, sending the T-ball rolling slowly toward third base. After several seconds of wild cheering, running, and throwing, the batter sits on first base in a cloud of dust. Safe!

Then an interesting thing happens. The kid scrambles to his feet and scans the crowd anxiously. Suddenly he beams. He spies his proud pop in the bleachers giving an enthusiastic thumbs-up.

This hunger to please our earthly parents is a reminder of the truth that we were created to honor our heavenly Father. Yet according to the promise above, we do this not by great exploits but by exercising simple faith. It's when we seek the Lord in hard times and trust him to see us through that we bring a smile to his face. Knowing that we've pleased him (even if our trials persist) is reward enough.

PRAYING GOD'S PROMISE

Without faith, God, I cannot please you. Forgive me for the times I wrongly imagine that you are pleased by my efforts for you. I demonstrate real faith by seeking after you, and you reward me amply. Give me a heart that is sincere. Give me a faith that is persistent, that continues to pursue you. Finding you is the great hope of my soul and the greatest reward I can imagine.

GOD'S PROMISE TO YOU

- Without faith you cannot please God.
- He rewards those who seek hard after him.

THE PROMISE
GOD REWARDS THOSE WHO HONOR HIM

> Let the Lord's people show him reverence, for those who honor him will have all they need. Even strong young lions sometimes go hungry, but those who trust in the Lord will never lack any good thing.
>
> Psalm 34:9-10

OLDER Bible translations speak often of "the fear of the Lord." Whatever does this phrase mean? Are we expected to cower with fright in God's presence? to live in continual terror and dread?

This kind of fear is the appropriate response of rebellious unbelievers who flaunt God's decrees. Having rejected almighty God as a merciful Savior, they now face the grim prospect of meeting him only in his role as the holy judge of the universe. On the other hand, for the beloved children of God, those whose sins have been forgiven by Christ, fearing God has a different connotation. The idea for believers is that of awe or stunned admiration in the presence of the great and good Creator. The implication is submissive reverence before a loving Lord. To "show him reverence" is to worship God above all other things. It involves the commitment to "honor" him and to "trust in" him.

Notice that the promise to the reverent is that God will meet all their needs. As God puts it in another verse, "I will honor only those who honor me" (1 Samuel 2:30).

PRAYING GOD'S PROMISE

You meet the needs of those who treat you with reverence, Lord. Forgive me for the times I fail to honor you. You are my friend, but you are also the majestic king of the universe, high and lifted up. As I trust in you, you fill my life with good things. Thank you for your care. I may not have all that my unredeemed human nature wants, but I do have all that my soul needs.

GOD'S PROMISE TO YOU

- God meets the needs of those who honor him.
- He makes sure his followers have good things.

THE PROMISE
GOD IS BIGGER THAN YOUR DILEMMAS

I am the Lord, the God of all the peoples of the world. Is
anything too hard for me? Jeremiah 32:27

Y OUR situation is grim. You feel lost in the dead end of a dark
maze. You ran out of options and "solutions" a long time ago.
You are past the point of exhaustion. Despair hovers over you
like a flock of hungry buzzards.

What you'd like, of course, is outright deliverance from your
difficulty. But at this point you'd settle for less spectacular help:
a fragment of wisdom, a speck of patience and strength, a small
bit of peace. You need grace for one more day, the ability to
endure without complaining. In short, you need the sustaining
touch of God.

If that or something like that describes where you are, the
divine promise above, with its bold rhetorical question, is the
verse you want rolling around in your head, heart, and soul. The
obvious implication is that nothing is too difficult for God, not
your external situation, not your internal confusion. Lost
causes are his specialty. The will of God, as the old saying goes,
will never take you where the grace of God cannot keep you.

PRAYING GOD'S PROMISE

You are the one true God, ruler of the heavens and the earth. When my faith is shaky, remind me of your power. Give me a fresh glimpse of who you really are. Nothing is impossible for you. Increase my faith, Lord. Supply the confidence I need to believe fully in this promise, especially when I am facing "hopeless" situations.

GOD'S PROMISE TO YOU

- God is the sovereign, almighty God.
- Nothing is too hard for him.

THE PROMISE
GOD PROMISES YOU ETERNAL TREASURE

His Holy Spirit speaks to us deep in our hearts and tells us that we are God's children. And since we are his children, we will share his treasures for everything God gives to his Son, Christ, is ours, too.   Romans 8:16-17

W HAT motivated explorers like Magellan and Columbus to sail across vast, uncharted oceans? What inspired scared young men to charge into the jaws of death on the beaches at Normandy? How do we explain missionaries, researchers, movie stars, or homemakers? The same way we explain a group of children digging a hole on a sandy beach. They are on a search for treasure.

This is what we are: nothing less than a race of treasure hunters. We individually pursue whatever we consider supremely valuable. If it's not the fortune of gold or silver or precious gems, then it's the "wealth" of freedom, fame, family, friendship, or . . . faith.

It's been said that nothing worth having is easy. If this is true, then maybe we can obtain the greatest treasures of all only through the greatest struggles. This might explain the great agonies of the Christian faith. And it also gives us a tantalizing hint of the phenomenal riches that await all of those who endure to the end.

PRAYING GOD'S PROMISE

As your child, Father, I am your heir. All that you have is mine! It is hard to fathom such a breathtaking promise. I am wealthy beyond words! Make this life-changing truth more than "head knowledge" to me. Cause it to sink deeply into my soul and to alter the way I live on a daily basis. I want to persevere for you.

GOD'S PROMISE TO YOU

- You are God's child.
- You will share all his treasures.

THE PROMISE
GOD IS INVOLVED IN YOUR LIFE

The steps of the godly are directed by the Lord. He delights in every detail of their lives. Though they stumble, they will not fall, for the Lord holds them by the hand.   Psalm 37:23-24

As we navigate our way through days filled with pain or sorrow or uncertainty, here's the straight skinny: There are no secret keys, no spiritual techniques, no super-duper prayers (not even the prayer of Jabez) that can guarantee us a Disneyesque happy ending in this life. That's because God's goal for us is not earthly bliss. It's something grander: his glory, brought about through our maturity.

We do well in tough times to forget about nonexistent magic wands and quick fixes and to focus on promises like the one above. Look at it closely. Notice what it claims: The living God directs the steps of his children. He is intimately involved in all the details of our lives. He holds us by the hand. And yes, he allows us to stumble.

Even so, we will not fall—at least not fatally. When we do trip, the Lord is there to pick us up and lead us further down the road.

PRAYING GOD'S PROMISE

I can't lie; I would love an easy life, Lord, one that is free of all trouble and grief and confusion. But you have never promised such an existence. In fact, the Bible tells me that I will go through hard times. Thank you for promising to direct me, to watch over me, to hold me by the hand. Give me wisdom and courage so that I am willing to walk with you wherever you lead.

GOD'S PROMISE TO YOU

- God directs your steps.
- He delights in the details of your life.
- He will not let you fall.

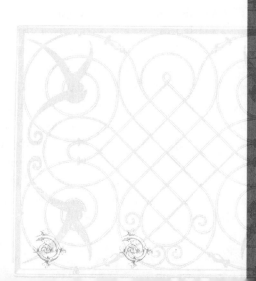

THE PROMISE
GOD WILL DESTROY THIS WORLD AND ALL
ITS TROUBLES

Then I saw a new heaven and a new earth, for the old heaven
and the old earth had disappeared. . . . I heard a loud shout
from the throne, saying, "Look, the home of God is now among
his people! He will live with them, and they will be his people.
God himself will be with them. He will remove all of their
sorrows, and there will be no more death or sorrow or crying
or pain. For the old world and its evils are gone forever."

Revelation 21:1-4

In the first century, while exiled on the barren island of Patmos,
the apostle John received this vivid glimpse of eternity.

Some call passages like this one "pie in the sky." But the children of God know that this snapshot of the future is anything
but wishful thinking. Our heavenly Father reigns. History, as the
old saying goes, is "His story." The day is coming when the
curtain will fall on this sin-scarred world. Finally and forever we
will see an end to sorrows, death, crying, and pain.

In the midst of our tough times we need to remember what
the future holds: not uncertainty and fear but the reassuring
promise of a brand-new existence void of bad things and filled
with God.

"Yes, dear friends, we are already God's children, and we can't even imagine what we will be like when Christ returns. But we do know that when he comes we will be like him, for we will see him as he really is" (1 John 3:2).

PRAYING GOD'S PROMISE

Come quickly, Lord Jesus! I praise you for your perfect ways, your perfect plan, and for the glorious future that awaits. Amen!

GOD'S PROMISE TO YOU

- God will bring an end to this old world and its troubles.
- He is preparing a heavenly home, where we will live together forever.

LEN WOODS is pastor of community life at Christ Community Church in Ruston, Louisiana. He is a former editor and writer at Walk Thru the Bible Ministries in Atlanta and is also the author of several books, including *Praise Notes* (Tyndale House, 1996), *The Unofficial Guide to Life after High School, Tough Choices: 52 Challenges Men Face, Life Application Family Devotions* (Tyndale House, 1997), and *I'm Outta Here: Facing Tough Choices after High School,* for which he won a Gold Medallion Award. He also contributed to the *Life Application Bible for Students* as well as the *Parents Resource Bible* and the *Praise and Worship Study Bible,* all published by Tyndale House.

Len dreams of one day making a hole in one, visiting the Holy Land, seeing the New Orleans Saints win the Super Bowl, and writing a best-selling novel—not necessarily in that order. Len and his wife have two sons and live in Ruston.

PRAYING GOD'S PROMISES SERIES